Six String Rocketeer

"Heartbreaking one moment, laugh-out-loud funny the next, *Six String Rocketeer* is a valuable book for anyone whose parents are going through a divorce. Without preaching, Jesse Butterworth invites readers into his own story of how he coped with his parents' breakup—and brings much-needed encouragement along the way."

—LEE STROBEL, author of *The Case for Christ* and *The Case for Faith*

"Jesse's transparency in communicating his story is refreshing, authentic, and powerful. Such bold honesty is missing from many of today's publications on the subject but was very present in the ministry of our Lord Jesus."

—GREGG GARNER, president/CEO, Global Outreach Developments International

"Anguish and pain and hope are all here. Jesse gives voice to the all-too-often silent children of divorce with biting wit and balanced wisdom."

—JOHN ORTBERG, teaching pastor, Menlo Park Presbyterian Church

"There is no easy way to weave a story of survival during the two most devastating things that can happen to a person—your parents' divorce and junior high. Butterworth pulls it off beautifully. The hope found here is tangible: hope for healing family relationships; hope for love that springs up through the cracks of the blacktop of pain; and hope for a song of victory that will finally be sung, rising higher than the voices of an eighth-grade choir, louder than the deafening silence of separation, and more glorious than a Six String Rocketeer."

—MIKE HOWERTON, author of *Miles to Cross,* coauthor
of *The Relevant Church,* Illuminate pastor

"As a child of divorce, I have Jesse's song 'Six String Rocketeer' on the soundtrack of my life. Now with his book, Jesse has crafted a poignant memoir, introducing readers to the important first step of acknowledging that parental divorce has lasting effects. His gracious approach and discerning insights invite readers to visit his past and, in the process, better understand their own."

—JEN ABBAS, author of *Generation Ex: Adult Children
of Divorce and the Healing of Our Pain*

"Jesse Butterworth is a passionate, real, and genuinely kind person. I've toured with him in the USA and in Europe and have seen him connect with people. He's interested in their stories and uses his own to bring understanding and healing. I've always loved the song 'Six String Rocketeer,' and after reading the book, I feel that I better understand his world and the world of those who have traveled a similar journey. Success for Jesse is using his life to touch others. I pray it touches millions."

—PAUL COLMAN, singer and songwriter

Six String Rocketeer

Six String Rocketeer

HOLDING LIFE TOGETHER
WHEN YOUR PARENTS SPLIT APART

Jesse Butterworth

WATERBROOK
PRESS

SIX STRING ROCKETEER
PUBLISHED BY WATERBROOK PRESS
12265 Oracle Blvd., Suite 200
Colorado Springs, Colorado 80921
A division of Random House, Inc.

Details in some anecdotes and stories have been changed to protect the identities of the
persons involved.

ISBN 1-57856-884-6

Copyright © 2005 by Jesse Butterworth

Published in association with the literary agency of Alive Communications, Inc.,
7680 Goddard Street, Suite 200, Colorado Springs, CO 80920.

Library of Congress Cataloging-in-Publication Data
Butterworth, Jesse.
   Six string rocketeer : holding life together when your parents split apart / Jesse
Butterworth. — 1st ed.
      p. cm.
   Includes bibliographical references.
   ISBN 1-57856-884-6
   1. Christian youth—Religious life. 2. Children of divorced parents—Religious life.
3. Butterworth, Jesse. I. Title.
   BV4531.3.B89 2005
   248.8'3—dc22

                                                    2005007775

Printed in the United States of America
2005—First Edition

10 9 8 7 6 5 4 3 2 1

To WaterBrook:
Thanks for taking a chance on this book.

To my family,
the most beautiful ball of dysfunction I've ever laid eyes on.
I love our times together. Thanks for letting me tell this story.
I couldn't have done it without you.
I love you all more today than I ever have.

To my wife,
the most beautiful creature I've ever laid eyes on.
You are my heart and soul. Thanks for your patience, your trust,
your support, and for saying "I do." I love you.

You and I
Brick and vine
Our spirits mesh
And intertwine.

To my God,
the most beautiful source of life one could ever experience.
Thanks for the Beatles, Elton John, Paul Simon,
James Taylor, Billy Joel, and the countless other musicians
who have touched my life so deeply.
Thanks for music. Thanks for family. And thanks for Jesus.
I love You with everything I've got,
and I hope I've made You proud.

Contents

Foreword

The first time I heard the song "Six String Rocketeer" I cried. Each time I have heard it subsequently, I have made every attempt to hold back the tears. Sometimes I succeed; sometimes I don't.

Today when I hear the song, my mind travels to two destinations. The first stop is a recording studio just outside of Nashville in early 2002. I was fortunate enough to hear the song recorded by the band named Daily Planet in their debut album for Reunion Records entitled *Hero*. Actually, I was there for the session in which they laid down the string section over the already-recorded drums, bass, guitar, and vocal tracks. I especially remember the cellos playing an uncanny recreation of the Beatles' hit "Eleanor Rigby." I recall the juxtaposition of feelings at that moment…feelings of pride in the songwriter's ability to communicate the message of empathy in pain and hope in healing, but also a feeling of overwhelming sadness.

And that feeling takes me to the second destination—the home in northern California where my kids grew up. For you see, "Six String Rocketeer" was written by Jesse Butterworth to convey the pain he encountered when his mother and father divorced.

And I am Jesse's father.

The most difficult days in our family's existence occurred in those months surrounding that divorce. At the time I thought no one could hurt as much as I did. But I've since come to realize there was plenty of pain to go around. I hurt. Jesse's brothers and sister hurt. His mom hurt. And Jesse hurt.

But his hurt led to his healing, and the crowning achievement of his young life was to write the words and music to "Six String Rocketeer." The song has touched thousands of young listeners, mostly sons and daughters whose mom and dad have divorced. The impact of this powerful ballad led to Jesse's being approached to expand his thoughts into book form.

And this is the book you hold in your hands. It is a gut-wrenchingly honest look at divorce through the eyes of one of its children. Jesse pulls no punches. There is no sugarcoating. It's not a fairy tale. It is not a cold, sterile, academic view of how young people cope with family breakdown. Rather, it is a young man's journey through the minefield of his own parents' divorce.

Granted, the book has moments that will make you laugh out loud. Jesse is a funny guy, and those of you who know me will read this book and quickly conclude Jesse was not adopted. His humor is contagious and comes at just the right times in the story.

But the book primarily addresses his pain and his wish to "just get away from it all." If you have endured or are enduring your parents' divorce, you will clearly identify and relate to him.

Above all, this book is a story of the pathway to healing. If your mom and dad have divorced, you will benefit by reading this book. You will empathize with Jesse's pain on every page. Both he and I pray you will also empathize with his process of healing. You *will* get through it. It *will* get better. God *will* help you. As Jesse writes in the song, "The wounds were deep inside my soul. Let the healing begin."

—Bill Butterworth
Jesse's dad,
author of New *Life After Divorce*

Prologue

T his is a book based on actual events. Some names have been changed, and some characters are a composite drawn from several individuals, but the heart of the story—as I remember it—is true.

Six String Rocketeer relates my experiences and how I recall them during the divorce of my parents. Please focus on what is written and avoid the temptation to make assumptions about what is not. Out of respect for my parents and my sister and brothers, I have intentionally not included many details and have not tried to tell the story from their individual perspectives.

Finally, over the years I have had hundreds of people ask me what I would suggest for kids stuck in the middle of a divorce. The truth is, I don't feel qualified to give advice since I am not a trained professional in the field of divorce recovery. But based on my experiences with my parents' divorce, here are some thoughts that may prove helpful:

- Make sure that you're communicating with God, your friends, your family, a journal, and a counselor. As I say in the book, silence can be a nasty habit. Try to stay on top of working through your thoughts and feelings. Keeping things bottled up inside will only hurt you in the long run.
- Look for productive outlets for your pain. For me it was music, but for you it may be pitching a baseball, dancing the tango, building a Web site, painting a picture, writing a story, or solving math equations. Whatever it is, find something

that excites you and pour yourself into it, not as a form of escapism, but as a tool for healing. Before you know it, your pain will become passion, and your misery will become music. It won't happen overnight, but as you grow and time passes, you will look back on your devotion to these personal interests and realize the wounds that hurt you really were the wounds that healed you.

I am honored that you would read this book and hope that you find it helpful, enjoyable, and thought provoking.

God's deepest blessings to you,
Jesse

The Wounds That Hurt You

T he airplane bounced between the orange and gray clouds. The
turbulence seemed to be rougher than normal, but I smiled
reassuringly at my beautiful blond companion. Nervous passengers
looked out the window, hoping to see the cause of the turbulence.
Our stomachs collectively went into our throats, and a flash of yellow
dropped in front of every seat as the plane lost thousands of feet of
altitude in an instant.

"Please do not panic! Secure your oxygen masks on your face as
demonstrated in preflight." The flight attendant's voice sounded like
Bob Dylan without his backup band—not a bit comforting. "However, if you are one of the many people who completely ignored me
during preflight instructions, I'm not going to tell you what you
should do in case of emergency! Good luck, you bottom-feeding
dung beetles!"

Dung Beetle

Noun. Any of various beetles of the family Scarabaeidae that form balls
of dung on which they feed and in which they lay their eggs.

Apparently sick of being ignored during her well-rehearsed, cheesy-joke-laden, preflight discourse, Diane, the flight attendant, had finally cracked.

Recognizing a golden opportunity to impress my gorgeous companion and win the respect of my elders and the adoration of my peers, I leaped from my seat, pushed Diane aside, and grabbed the conch to take control. Of course, being only twelve years old, I realized gaining control of the passengers would be an uphill battle, but it was a battle I was willing to fight.

"Quiet, please," I said slowly and smoothly through the hand-held. My voice sounded much deeper and authoritative through the mike. "Worry not, my weary travelers. My name is Jesse Butterworth, and I am here to save the day." The chaos turned to silence as the hushed crowd waited for my next calming syllable. "Please do not panic. Everything is under control." I caught the eye of my companion, and she smiled adoringly in my direction.

As soon as calm had been restored to the cabin, the pilot rushed out of the cockpit in a flustered state. "Please, please," he begged. "Does anyone here know how to fly this plane? I'll never be able to land in weather this bad!"

This statement was met with fearful screams from the panicked passengers.

"Have no fear, Pilot," I said in deep, rich tones. "I hold the second highest score on my Nintendo flight-simulator game, so I'm sure I'll be able to land this baby."

The pilot heard none of this, because he had curled into a fetal position and had begun sucking his thumb.

I stepped over the pilot, opened the door to the cockpit, and nestled into the pilot's seat. I took stock of all the controls in front of me:

there were hundreds of lights and buttons, but there was only one place for steering. Like the single bead of sweat that hung from the tip of my nose, this plane would fall out of the sky if I did not gain control. I grabbed the violently shaking stick and tried with all my might to steady the craft. My muscles swelled until my shirt began to rip across my arms and chest. With one last burst of pure, unadulterated strength, I steadied the plane, and with the finesse of a Blue Angel pilot, I steered that baby to safety.

The passengers were chanting my name in victory.

"Butterworth! Butterworth! Butterworth!"

And I even did it with my eyes closed.

CRASHING INTO REALITY

"Butterworth!" Mr. Grant snapped.

I opened my eyes and discovered that I was still sitting in Mr. Grant's English class. To say this was a letdown is a huge understatement.

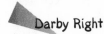

Darby Right

On the first day of school, Darby Right was so grieved to be in Mr. Grant's English class that he made it his life's mission to get re-assigned to a different class. By doing these five little things, he found success:

1. Replacing Mr. Grant's cherished dry erase markers with permanent markers
2. Incessantly humming "Shipoopie" from *The Music Man*
3. Shouting, "Here! Oh, sorry, not me," after every single name on the roll was called

4. Insisting he had double vision and needed two copies of every handout

5. Replacing Mr. Grant's teacher's edition with his own student edition in which he had written bogus answers in red ink. Mr. Grant didn't catch on until halfway through the period when he realized that the feuding families in *Romeo and Juliet* were called the Poo-Poos and the Pee-Pees.

I had successfully tuned out Mr. Grant's droning voice long enough to save the day on that ill-fated flight but not long enough to last the entire period. This was not unusual behavior for me. When I wanted to escape, I would climb into my brain and find someplace else to go. I blinked hard and looked at Sunny Gersbach, the beautiful blonde to my right. Sunny was a sight to behold. Her long hair lay perfectly on her shoulders, she had the eyes of a Hello Kitty, and the perma-tan color of her skin was a perfect hue. I looked down at her desk—at the pages of notes that grew by the minute—and my crush on her grew by the second. The only foreseeable problem was that she didn't know I existed. There had to be a way to gain the affection of the most sought-after girl in the eighth grade even if I was a nobody.

I always parted my white-blond hair from right to left, laying it against my cowlick to create a natural Superman curl on my forehead. I was a chubby kid (though I preferred the term *stocky*, because it made me sound more athletic) who was trying to find his own sense of humor in a world of sarcastic students. At that point the only way I was able to get laughs was to repeat something funny the quiet kid behind me had said. The louder I said it, the funnier it was, but I was only as good as the student behind me.

The other thing I didn't have going for me was the last name of

Butterworth. Imagine being chubby and having that name. It's like living with a giant bull's-eye painted on your back.

Talking Syrup Bottles

Spare me, please. I've heard every known joke about my last name. Yes, my mom is a talking syrup bottle. Yes, my aunt is Jemima. Yes, my uncle is Ben. I've heard them all. It's pretty remarkable when people ask me if I've ever heard of Mrs. Butterworth's syrup. Sometimes, just for fun, I pretend that I haven't and tell the unknowing person that the coincidence is quite comical. I once had a grocery clerk stop in the middle of checking my groceries and get on the loudspeaker to ask someone to bring her a bottle of the syrup just to show me it really did exist. When she got the bottle, I just continued to play dumb about the whole thing because I felt so bad.

Eying the clock, I noticed there were only a few minutes remaining in the period, so I picked up my pencil, reopened my *Fresh Prince of Bel-Air* Trapper Keeper, and jotted down the notes that Mr. Grant had scrawled on the dry erase board.

Mr. Grant usually littered the board with barely legible chicken scratching that he copied verbatim out of the teacher's edition of the text. To this day I sincerely believe the greatest joy Mr. Grant found in each day of teaching was getting high off the smell of his dry erase markers. Perhaps on this day Mr. Grant had taken one too many whiffs of his Magic Markers, because the board was stark empty except for these fourteen words:

The wounds that hurt you would be the wounds that would heal you. —Unknown

I clicked my mechanical pencil a couple of times to get some fresh lead out and wrote that quote down. It had piqued my interest, but I was quite certain that either Mr. Grant hadn't a clue what it meant, or he had explained it while I was saving the world in my head. I would have to figure it out for myself.

The God Squad

The anticipated bell rang. My detested fourth-period English class was over, and the adored lunch period had begun. I packed up my things and headed to my usual lunch spot, where the rest of my friends had already congregated. We were a group of guys who found ourselves somewhere in the middle of the food chain. We weren't the misfits or the unpopulars, but we weren't the athletes, the kids with mustaches, or the populars, either. We were often referred to as the "God Squad" because we were all church kids. But it wasn't our deep love for the unlovely, our hours donated to charity, or our total abandonment to Jesus that set us apart. It was that we didn't cuss. We avoided every forbidden four-letter word by substituting words like *frigging* and *schista* and using phrases such as "What the crap!" Also, if we ever said something negative about a person, we began by saying, "Bless her heart," and then followed it up with something like, "but Janet is truly the most repulsive girl in the whole school."

Clearly we were setting a truly Christlike example for our fellow students.

The group consisted of five guys: Ted, Nater, Randy, Aaron, and me.

The God Squad

Name: Ted Encotti

Nickname: T-bone

Stats: T-bone was a stout Italian kid with earlobes you could use for pillows. He had black, curly hair that 'froed around eleven thirty every day because his hair product just wasn't up to the job. He was a good-spirited kid, but he was insecure about his weight and would look for any way to get the attention off himself and onto somebody else. His parents were strict and would make him do Bible studies when he disobeyed them. His greatest fear was that he would grow up to be his father, a stern and religious man who had no idea how to tell his son that he loved him.

Name: Nathan Fallstream

Nickname: Nater

Stats: Nater was the ringleader of the God Squad. His voice had changed in seventh grade, he had once kissed a girl on the cheek and the corner of her lips, and there were rumors that T-bone had seen some armpit hair on Nater when they were swimming before school started. He had brown hair cut in the popular style, his ears stuck out slightly, his big brown eyes were trustworthy, and his acne was barely noticeable. He always had cool clothes and went to every Sacramento Kings game, because his dad was a season-ticket holder. In the world of eighth grade, 98 percent of our stock went into looks and style. Therefore, Nater became our fearless leader.

Name: Randy Wackerly
Nickname: Stick
Stats: Randy was sort of an odd duck. He looked like a broom full of bright red bristles. He was skinny as a rake (hence the nickname) and had bright red hair that could land a plane on a foggy night. He had to safety-pin his turtlenecks so they would look form fitting.

He had perfectly straight teeth because he had worn braces and headgear for years. But instead of wearing the headgear only at night like most kids, Stick thought he would speed up the process by wearing it around the clock. (Of course, the only clocks in his house were powered by potatoes because of his undying love for science.)

When I first met him, I thought he was a special-needs kid. But he wasn't. He was just Stick.

Name: Aaron Kent
Nickname: none
Stats: Aaron looked like an all-American kid. He had thick brown hair neatly parted in the middle, framing his freckled face. He was book smart and as nice as they come. He had an old soul—the kind of soul that made you want to sit under his tree for a while and catch a nap in the shade.

He had an old vocabulary, too. His grandma lived with his family, and her influence would come out every so often when we'd hear him say things like "Good night shirt!" and "Jiminy Christmas!"

Aaron was pure. That's what everybody liked about him.

I took part in our usual conversations about baseball, Nintendo, and girls, but I had a burden I wanted to share with someone, baggage that had been hanging heavy on my heart. I felt I could trust my friends with something this serious.

"I think my parents are going to get a divorce," I said without any warning.

"What?" Nater yelped.

"I said I think my parents might be getting a divorce."

"Did they tell you they are getting a divorce?" Aaron asked.

"No, but my sister, my brothers, and I can hear them fighting all the time in their bedroom. They never used to fight this much. It seems like they're going to get a divorce," I answered.

"I thought your dad was a Christian speaker and stuff. Didn't he write a book about families? How can he be getting a divorce?" T-bone asked in a partly bewildered and partly pointed tone.

"Well, he is, but…I…they're…" I could feel the lump in my throat grow as I tried to defend my parents, and I knew if I uttered another word, it would be Niagara Falls.

I couldn't explain to these guys what had happened. In fact, to this day I can't explain how or why my parents' marriage failed. I just knew that I hated going home and pretending that everything was okay.

"Well, if they didn't tell you that they're going to, then maybe they're not. I mean, why cut off your nose despite your face."* Aaron was the only one of my friends whose parents were divorced. He was also the only one who not only used sayings in the wrong context but screwed them up altogether—yet another fingerprint of his grandmother's effect on his speech.

"Yeah," I said as I tried to pull myself together and make myself invisible.

> ***Correct saying:** Cut off your nose to spite your face
> **Definition:** Disadvantage yourself to harm your adversary

Unpacking the Baggage

After we talked awhile longer about secret levels on Super Mario Bros. 3, the bell rang, and we separated to attend our afternoon classes.

Special Secret Mario Message

Defeat the Koopaling at the end of an Airship (Worlds 1-7) while wearing either the Frog, Tanooki, or Hammer Brothers suit and receive a special message from the King.

Sitting in Mr. Flinger's science class, I played the divorce scenario through my head. How could my family be crumbling? Although his response seemed rather piercing, T-bone did have a point. My dad was a Christian author, and he spoke all around the country on family values and togetherness. My mom had gone to church since we were little, and she loved her family. It just didn't add up. How could this be happening?

2

Roll with the Punches

The May sun shone through the pine trees, illuminating the dust kicked up by Janitor Joe's omnipresent leaf blower. The rays reminded me that the end of my eighth-grade year was approaching. I absolutely dreaded the month of May. Not because of the final tests, the proficiency exams, the papers, or the class projects. The reason I despised May was that it was basketball month in gym class.

Being from a family of five kids (Joy, Jesse, Jeffrey, John, and Joseph), I was no hack with the hoop. Although my short, stocky build might suggest otherwise, I was a pretty good jumper. When I would soar through the air, it was often impossible to tell me from the basketball, but that is neither here nor there. My point is that being embarrassed about my playing ability was not the reason I loathed the month of May.

Jungle Ball

Our hoop at home backed up against a wooded decline, so every time we missed a shot, we had to go hiking into a downhill wilderness. Sick of the poison oak we got from retrieving the ball, we became pretty good shots.

I had once heard of the existence of two dozen red jerseys and two dozen white jerseys that could easily split a class into two teams. However, our sadistic gym teacher, Mr. Flinger, insisted we play shirts and skins. *Shirts and skins!* This, my friends, is why I detested the month of May.

Shirtless Evil

Junior high is a rough time as it is. It's as if once you reach the eighth grade, your vision is impaired so that all you can see are the things that make you different from others and not the things you have in common or that make each of us unique. I'm sure if we really examined all the common bonds at that age (zits, love for *Saturday Night Live,* hormones, Game Boy, insecurities, etc.), we would have no problem finding things to talk about. Unfortunately, we not only begin to notice the things that separate us, but we sniff them out and bring them to the surface.

Each May morning I would pray that the Lord would spare me the humiliation of having to play shirtless in front of my peers, giving them yet another reason to poke fun at me. For two weeks the Lord heard my prayers and delivered me from that shirtless evil. One fateful Friday all that changed.

Wearing our way-too-short green gym shorts and our never-been-washed-once gray gym shirts, we shuffled to the outdoor basketball courts.

"Fresh Out of the Dryer" Smell

Every day after gym class we balled up our sweaty, gray gym shirts and shoved them into our lockers. The next day we unraveled the reeking, crusty mass and massaged it into something that resembled a shirt. We were supposed to take our shirts home once a week to wash them, but we came up with a new way to give them that "fresh out of the dryer" smell. We took our sticks of deodorant and rubbed them all over our shirts. You had to stay away from chalky deodorants, because they left a tacky, white residue all over your shirt, making it look like you washed it in cottage cheese. You always wanted to go with the clear sports sticks.

Yes, it was sick but, oh, so effective.

Our clumsy herd of self-consciousness lined up on the blacktop in alphabetical order and awaited our fate.

With clipboard in hand, the infamous Mr. Flinger walked in front of our shipshape line like Patton before his troops. By the emphatic tone in his voice and the slightly maniacal grin on his face, it was quite obvious he was enjoying this a little too much.

Finger Flinger

Mr. Fred Flinger also taught science class.

During a week of studying human growth and development, he lectured on a baby's first month of life. Deconstructing the effects of jaundice (why a baby may look yellow or orange like a carrot after it's born), he explained that too much bilirubin (pronounced bill-uh-roo-bin) in a baby's body is the reason for the change in appearance. Much to Mr. Flinger's delight, there was a kid named Billy Reuben in the class. Pointing out the obvious connection that "Billy Reuben" and "bilirubin" sound similar, Mr. Flinger ensured that Billy's nickname from that day on was Jaundice.

Not going down without a fight, Jaundice—er, I mean Billy—gave Mr. Flinger a moniker of his own. It was no secret that Mr. Flinger

enjoyed mining for gold in his own nostrils without the use of a
Kleenex or hanky. Seeing a perfect opportunity to pounce, Billy gave
Mr. Flinger the nickname he could never shake: Finger Flinger.

As Mr. Flinger moved right through the A's and headed straight for
the B's, I threw up a Hail Mary prayer and offered my life as a Bible
translator to the indigenous tribes of Peru if the Lord would spare me
the humiliation of having to shed my shirt in front of my peers.

Head Reducers

There are several tribes indigenous to Peru. The Jíbaros, for example,
used to decapitate their enemies, empty their skulls of brains, and
then fill them with hot sand. Eventually the heads would shrink because
of the heat, and the shrunken heads would become trophies.

"Butterworth…" Time slowed as Mr. Flinger wagged his Her-
man Munster–like index finger at me and said the word that made
my bowels retreat to my ankles: "Skins."

I wrung my green shorts with my large-palmed hands and looked
to the heavens, wondering why the Peruvians didn't need another
Bible translator.

"Please, Mr. Flinger…," I tried to plead, but he ignored me and
moved down the roll sheet to his next shirtless sap.

THE ESCAPE HATCH

Fortunately, my procrastinating nature had temporarily given way to
a night of preparation. I had played this moment over and over in my
head the night before.

Fake an aneurysm?

Pull a hammy?

Wet my pants?

Standing there like a deer in headlights, I couldn't bring myself to use any of these escape hatches.

Fortunately, I had a backup plan for my backup plan. Standing in front of my mirror the night before, mentally preparing for such a time as this, I realized that my saving grace just might be the very shirt on my back. I would have to take it off if I were cast into the savage skins nation. However, what if there was a way to only *half* take off my shirt?

By keeping my arms through the armholes, I could pull the shirt over my head and behind my neck to create a sort of bro (a male bra). My polar white tummy would signify my allegiance to my teammates, while my brittle, gray T-shirt would hide my baby-fat boobies.

The Bro

This term was popularized by the *Seinfeld* episode "The Doorman,"
which originally aired February 23, 1995. The episode is popularly
referred to as "The Bro" or "The Manssiere."

After he had determined the fate of Timmy Zimmer, I ran to Mr. Flinger with my newly transformed T-shirt/bra and begged him to let me wear it. Trying not to crack a smile and reveal that he had a rarely seen softer side, Mr. Flinger allowed me to wear my shirt as a modified bro for the duration of the game.

"Come on, Jesse. Let's go!" Aaron called from the other side of the court. Aaron was a fellow skin and a pretty good player himself.

"Here, pass it in," he said as he handed me the ball.

I passed the ball in, and the game was on.

Much to my disbelief, it seemed to be going well. As long as I could stay virtually invisible on the court and get rid of the ball as soon as I got it, my plan just might work.

BUTTERBALL

"Nice pass, Butterworth."

"Way to keep it alive, Jesse!"

I was beginning to feel like a part of the team. Thinking of the basketball as a ticking time bomb in my hands, I had racked up a number of assists. I was moving the ball so well that my teammates were actually passing the ball my way!

The girls' PE class was doing its daily jog around the school and began its loop around the blacktop in the middle of our game. Between hoops I caught a glorious glimpse of my golden-haloed goddess, Sunny. Sweat dewed on her face, giving the sun even more cause for envy.

Feeling like an active, contributing member of this ragtag group of half-naked warriors, I knew this could be my golden moment to shine in front of the unknowing object of my affection. As if he had read my mind, the magic hands of Bobby Reimboldt tossed the ball to me, leading me to the basket. The pass was over my head by design, and my uncanny leaping ability sprang into action (literally) as I reached over my head to acquire this little slice of splendor.

With my playground-dirty hands reaching for the ball, I came to the horrifying realization that I had not taken this particular circumstance into consideration. By reaching my arms well over my head, the tension pulled my makeshift bro from its proper positioning, exposing my boobies to the peering public. I quickly retracted my hands to reposition my homemade boulder holder, letting the ball go out of bounds.

This was not a smart move.

Not only had I been exposed, but I had drawn the attention of both teams.

"Nice boobs, Butterball!" Three words that make me wake up in a cold sweat to this day.

"Yeah, why don't you wear a bra?"

Like a pack of wolves in a frenzied state, my classmates had turned against me and let their underage angst come out to play.

I turned to the glowing yellow light to my left and saw Sunny Gersbach looking at me in my moment of deepest disgrace.

I had to do something to get the attention off me.

I thought as quickly as I could. Sharp comebacks and distracting jokes eluded me.

Fake an aneurysm?

Pull a hammy?

Wet my pants?

In a moment of weakness, I found the escape hatch I had been looking for: my friend and teammate T-bone.

T-bone was the only boy in eighth grade who had bigger chest mounds than I did and the only boy who was more insecure about it. In an act of utter, utter desperation that I regret to the very day I write these words, I blurted out, "Oh yeah? You think these are big? Look at Teddy's! Those make Dolly Parton's look like a little girl in a training bra!"

The taunting spotlight quickly left me and pointed at T-bone. Like Dorothy dumping water on the Wicked Witch, I watched T-bone melt in disgrace into the blacktop. Tears filled his eyes as he crossed his arms over his chest and hunched his back in defeat.

Seeing that play had stopped, Finger Flinger removed his pointer finger from his nostril and gave a *toot-toot* on his whistle. The sharp shriek of the whistle got the boys' minds back on playing ball and off T-bone and me. The game continued, but I had lost all ability to play. The nausea eating at my insides kept me from doing anything useful.

I had successfully diverted the taunts of the jeering mob but at the price of alienating one of my closest friends.

I was sure T-bone would later forgive me for sicking the wolves on him, but how could I have done that? When all we're looking for is a place to belong, how could I push someone so close to me outside the circle?

The Hulk

With the attention off him, T-bone pulled himself together. In a move that surprised everyone on that steaming asphalt, he turned from embarrassed little boy into angered beast. Dr. Banner was sick of being walked all over, and it was time to let the Hulk come out and play.

As the shirts brought the ball down the court, T-bone turned his humiliation into rage. He not only played defense. He became the defense.

Moving his arms in all directions, he downed the offense like a bowling ball crushing a LEGO castle.

With the other team's offense defeated, T-bone began to look for anyone else still standing.

His teammates were fleeing from King Kong, but I stood in

place, paralyzed by the shock and awe of the mighty display of power I had just seen. He saw me out of the corner of his eye and let his wrath fly.

There was a blur of gray and green, a sharp pain in my stomach, and a swift meeting of my bare knees with the cruel blacktop.

The feeling of guilt that had infested my stomach was quickly replaced with the sting of the sword of retribution.

Take My Breath Away

The solar plexus, located just below the center of the rib cage, is a very sensitive area. A strike to this zone causes the diaphragm, which is the muscle that controls lung inflation and deflation, to spasm. One is unable to take a breath until the diaphragm returns to normal.

CALLING THE CATTLE BACK

Sitting next to Aaron on the bus ride home that afternoon, I ran the events through my mind.

"No offense, Jesse, but what you did to T-bone was not cool, man," Aaron said.

"Yeah, I know. I feel like such a chump."

"It sounds a little bit like the pot calling the cattle back."* There was yet another remnant of Aaron's grandma. Although it was an incorrect adage, I knew what he was trying to say.

> ***Correct saying:** The pot calling the kettle black
> **Definition:** The accuser is as guilty as the accused

"Yeah, I don't know what to tell you," I said as I tried to pick the tiny pieces of asphalt out of my wounded knees. "I just panicked and didn't know what else to do."

"Can you believe T-bone, though?" Aaron asked. "I think he had finally had enough. He just snapped."

The bus had been abuzz with the legend of T-bone. He was Magnolia Junior High's very own Braveheart.

As I limped off the bus at my stop, I actually heard a sixth grader say, "I heard that he whupped fifty eighth graders with his bare hands."

I smiled slightly and headed home.

3

Caught in the Crossfire

My calf muscles burned from walking up the hill as I headed home from the bus stop. My skinned-up knees seemed to have a heartbeat of their own, but that pain was no match for how bad I felt about turning on T-bone. I was looking forward to getting home and hiding from my troubles for a while.

I grabbed the mail out of the mailbox and pulled the garbage can up the driveway before entering the house.

Refuse the Refuse

The garbage was my chore around the house. I often forgot to take the trash can to the curb on trash night and spent many an early morning flagging the garbagemen down, begging them to turn around and empty our refuse. On one occasion, after missing the trashmen two weeks in a row, we had an overflowing can of trash that could hold no more. Knowing I would get in big trouble if I missed another week, I pulled the trash can down to the curb at 4:30 a.m. after the sound of the garbage truck had awakened me. The garbagemen were long gone by the time I finally got the can to the curb, so I did the only thing I could think of. I wheeled the can over to what looked like a wooded area and dumped it. In the pitch black of night, the garbage was nicely concealed under the trees and pine needles.

Later, when I was walking down to the bus stop, I realized that I hadn't dumped the trash in a wooded area at all. I had dumped it down our neighbor's unswept driveway. Unfortunately, I had to clean it up, fess up to what I'd done, and run to the bus stop to catch the bus. I tried to wash my filthy hands as quickly as I could, but in my haste I pumped the lotion bottle instead of the soap dispenser. I couldn't rinse all the lotion off my hands, so for the rest of the day I smelled like a peachy apricot covered in two-week-old Indian food.

Why do people put the lotion right next to the soap?

Walking in the front door, I saw my siblings, Joy, Jeffrey, John, and Joseph, already home and watching TV in the family room.

SIBLING REVELRY

Name: Joy
Age: 14
Stats: Joy is the only girl among the Butterworth kids. The oldest of five kids, her role became peacekeeper and warden of fair play. For example, if only two doughnuts were left, Joy would meticulously cut them into five equal

pieces so that we could all enjoy the same amount. She also became quite good at breaking up fights between brothers without getting hit herself. She was Mom #2 to my younger brothers. With five kids, my mom had a hard time keeping up, so my sister would often step in and fill the gap.

Joy is an unlikely fit in a family fueled by humor, but what she lacks in wit she makes up in heart. She loves her family more than anything else, and she hates conflict more than anything else. On her tenth birthday, while opening gifts like a jump rope and socks, she broke down in tears, thinking of the day, years from that one, when she would grow up and leave her house, her family, and everything she held so dear.

When we were younger, we'd perform original musicals in the backyard. Joy's character would always be a nineteenth-century prairie dweller who carried a ragged broom and sang songs like this:

> *Mom and Dad went off to war*
> *So I am left here to raise my orphaned brothers*
> *Sweeping the chimney.*
> *Oh, how I sweep the chimney.*

She was tall and thin, had long, blond hair, and hadn't realized how pretty she was.

Name: Jeffrey

Age: 10

Nickname: JEB (his initials) or Jebby

Stats: Clearly the most artistic of the kids, Jeffrey enjoyed drawing cartoon characters and giving them names and entire histories. This came in handy later when, for one of his school projects, he was supposed to write a paper about someone on the police force. Instead of actually finding someone, he made up an uncle named Gene Fogelberg who was part of the police force of Kennebunkport, Maine. I have to admit, that report was far more fascinating than any other report I've ever read.

He is the middle child and had avoided being the black sheep until this point in his life. He had loads of passion that had to be put into something, whether it was art, sports, or relationships. Without a place to put it, he was like a bazooka without aim.

Although he was shy, he always relished his time in the spotlight. He was known for doing intriguing little things, like carving the letters RHD into the bricks over the fireplace (we still have no idea what RHD means), dropping spoons into holes in the wall, and taking John's imaginary friend, Dokey, hostage for an afternoon.

He is directly under me in birth order, and therefore we fought like there was no tomorrow. If it hadn't been for Joy pulling us apart, we probably would have beaten each other like rented mules.

Name: John

Age: 7

Stats: When they say that kids are made of rubber, they must have John in mind. He used to ride downhill sitting on a skateboard and stop himself with his bare feet. He would stand up—unscathed—grab his skateboard, and head back up the hill to do it again. He once came into the house with blood all over him because half of his chin was no longer connected to his face. He had been kneeling on his skateboard, doing a downhill slalom, when he hit a bump and got a face full of gravel. I'd have been bawling like a baby, but not John. He was tough as nails. He just stood there with an expression on his face like he was try-ing to recall the punch line to a funny joke he had heard earlier.

John was a nice, eager-to-please kid, which didn't get you very far in this family.

When it came time for hand-me-downs, John always got one of two things: tiny belly shirts that would make Britney Spears blush or polo shirts that belonged to Big Bird before he molted. He gladly took either one and went on his merry way.

He has a dry, off-the-cuff sense of humor and was unknowingly the author of some of my best jokes. I would hear him say something funny at home and then pass it off at school as if I were a regular stand-up comedian, but the real funnyman was my brother John.

Name: Joseph

Nickname: **Bo** *(My mom didn't want us to call him Joe for short, so we had to come up with something else.)*

Age: 4

Stats: The baby of the Butterworth bunch, Bo saw few hard days. His life began in a womb so stretched out by four predecessors that his idea of a fetal position was spread-eagle, flailing his arms freely. He was well loved and well taken care of. Of course, after he grew up, we made a slave out of him, but when he was little, he was the cutest thing you'd ever seen: a fivehead (that's one bigger than a fore-head) a Klingon warrior would be jealous of, eyes that were always looking for someone to emulate, ears always listening for a good story, a mouth that loved to smile, and, of course, those cheeks. In the world of cute, there are chubby cheeks, and then there are Joseph cheeks. Those things were so soft, smooth, and full that he must have considered them a curse. We pinched his cheeks every time we saw him. Eventually, tired of always having sore cheeks, he'd give you the look of death followed by a stern, "Shtop it!" if you even made a move toward his face.

Being the youngest, he never knew just how good he had it. By the time he was in junior high, he was wearing all new, brand-name clothing. When I was in junior high, I was still wearing XJ-900s from Payless Shoe Source—the really bad knockoffs of the latest Air Jordans. Man, Bo had it good.

WEAPON OF MASS DISTRACTION

They all looked up from the TV, shell-shocked. I assumed they were dumbfounded by the acting (if you want to call it that) of Screech in the comedy (if you want to call it that) *Saved by the Bell.*

Dumb as a Bell

The answer: The junior-high gang that started out at school in Indiana and then turned up the next season in the same school, except with a different name, in California

The question: Who is the cast of *Saved by the Bell*?

I dropped my backpack by the door, put the mail on the dining-room table, and headed to the kitchen to get an after-school snack. I grabbed a Fruit Roll-Up, went back into the family room, and sat next to Jebby on the couch. No one said a word; they just kept watching a commercial for the new Smurfs Shrinky Dinks as if it were an enthralling epic.

Hypocritical Mass

We once had a rather large baby-sitter who never allowed us to watch *The Smurfs* or *He-Man*. She had once heard that the names Gargamel and Azrael were taken from the satanic bible and that whenever Adam became He-Man by the "power of Grayskull," it was somehow satanic too. But for some reason, this lady was cool with letting us watch such "classics" as Tom and Jerry and the Road Runner and Wile E. Coyote. She'd much rather we watch two animals scheme different ways to completely obliterate each other than watch cartoons that had vague references to a book we'd never pick up in our lifetimes.

The TV was blaring. The song for the commercial ended, and there were five seconds of silence, and I found out why the TV was so loud and why everyone was watching it intently.

A loud noise came from down the hall—loud enough for me to recognize my mother's voice but too muffled to decipher what was being said. I heard my dad answer in an angry and even louder tone. I made eye contact with Joy. Without any words we said to each other, *Not again.*

This had become a daily event. It started out just once in a great while, and then it was more like once a month, then twice a month, then once a week, and now almost every day. For whatever reason, the arguing got especially bad around dinnertime.

Like a battalion of soldiers pinned down in a foxhole, we were caught in the cross fire while the battle raged down the hall. We were a poorly armed militia that lacked the tools to deal with this kind of battle. The only weapon we had was the WMD—the weapon of mass distraction. We looked for anything to keep our minds off the marriage unraveling twenty feet away behind closed doors. The two people we loved and trusted more than anyone else in the world were trying to figure out if they loved each other anymore. The united front was breaking apart.

SILENCE IS AN AWFUL HABIT

The commercial break ended, and the show resumed. Zack had sneaked into Mr. Belding's office with the tank-topped Slater close behind. I hated this show. I always had. But like my sister and brothers, I stared intently at the screen, trying to block out all noises other than those coming from the TV.

We sat through two more mind-numbing episodes before Joy broke the silence and asked what had happened to my knees. She was in high school, so she hadn't heard the legend of T-bone yet. I told her that I ate it on the blacktop and that it was no big deal.

She nodded and went back to watching TV.

I wanted to tell her the whole story about being on the skins team, getting made fun of, humiliating my friend, and getting socked in the stomach for it, but I found it easier to say nothing.

Silence, I learned, is an awful habit.

The door to my parents' room opened, and my mom burst through it. She wiped the tears from her face and walked into the family room. "Joy, can you start browning the ground beef, please?" she asked.

Without a word, my sister got up and went into the kitchen.

"Jesse, did you bring the trash can up from the curb?"

"What?" I asked, even though I'd heard what she'd said. For some reason, once I turned twelve, my natural reflex was to respond to whatever my parents were saying with the question "What?"

"Did you bring the trash can up?" she repeated.

"Yeah."

Around my parents I was a man of few words. What would we talk about, anyway? They wouldn't understand my life at school, and since they had started fighting all the time, I wanted to be as far away from them as possible.

"Okay." She forced a smile and headed for the kitchen.

My dad came out of their bedroom toweling off his freshly washed face. His hands were still shaking, his face was still red, and his chin still quivered from the bedroom conflict.

"How you doing, buddy?" he asked me as he sat down on the couch.

"What?" I asked.

"What happened to your knees?"

"Nothing. I just fell in gym class."

At that point I could no longer stand to be in the same room with either of my parents. They were not making my already difficult life any easier, and I didn't want to have anything to do with them.

"Homework," I said as I stood up. I grabbed my backpack and headed for my bedroom.

I saw my dad's chin quiver again as I passed him, but at that point in my life I couldn't deal with any more complexities. I just wanted it simple.

FASTER THAN A SPEEDING BUTTERBALL

I plopped my backpack down on the floor of my bedroom and fell backward onto my bed. I stared up at my walls, which were covered with an array of posters, from Bo Jackson to the Justice League of America.

JLA

When the first issue of *Justice League of America* debuted on comic stands in the early 1960s, its members included Superman, Batman, Wonder Woman, the Flash, Green Lantern, Martian Manhunter, and Aquaman. The issue was called "Brave and the Bold" and told the story of the JLA fighting an evil, gigantic, telepathic starfish named Starro who was out to conquer the world.

I looked at a poster of the Flash, the fastest human in the world, and was inspired by his super speed. I burst through the door of my room and ran down the driveway—and just kept running. I ran by T-bone's house and apologized. I ran by Sunny Gersbach's house to show her I was indeed good at something. I ran by Mr. Flinger's house and pantsed him while he was picking his nose. I ran down Highway 49, and soon I was traveling faster than cars, sound, light, and, most important, my troubles. I ran through the mountains, stretching out my arms to feel the cool evening breeze tickle my fingertips. I leaped off the edge of a mountain and flew over my town, looking at everything from a bird's-eye view. Life was much simpler up there. The world was just a series of lines and dots. I could see my house, and it looked peaceful, nestled in a hill among the mighty pine trees.

"Dinnertime!" John yelled through my door in his high-pitched voice.

With that, I was instantly transported from ten thousand feet above my home back onto my bed.

"What?" I said, opening my eyes wide.

"Come and get it," John said as he walked away from the door and toward the dining room.

Great. Just what I need, I thought. *An awkward dinner full of forced smiles and small talk. Maybe they'll let me eat dinner in my room.*

I opened my bedroom door and walked back into the thickened air of the house, the type of air that made every move just a little harder to make, and every breath just a little harder to breathe.

Blasting Off

A nd so it arrived on a hot June day: eighth-grade graduation. For some students this day was as slow in arriving as stubborn ketchup that won't come out no matter how hard you shake the bottle. For others it came as fast as the end of a great movie. For me, it was somewhere in between. I was glad to have the school part over, but I also liked having a place to go during the day. The way things were going at home, this summer could be a long one.

The baseball field in front of the school had been converted for a grand commencement celebration, and the blacktop (pieces of which were still embedded in my knees) had become an overflow parking lot. Gray metal folding chairs lined the freshly mowed outfield, and American flags punctuated each row with an exclamation point. Anxious parents, relatives, and friends scuttled in from the steaming blacktop to the moist grass, looking to snag the closest seat in order to get the best pictures of their little graduate.

I hoped that my folks would be sitting close to get pictures of me in my sweet new getup. I was decked out in a rad green rayon shirt, a Jerry Garcia tie, and pleated black dress pants. Yes, my friends, I was ready to graduate in style. Shorts and a T-shirt probably would have been a more appropriate choice, because the northern California summer temperatures were already reaching into the midnineties, and there was no shade in the middle of a baseball diamond. It would be a sweltering evening, but the temperature wasn't my biggest concern. Knowing full well that I get sunburned from looking at a fluorescent light, I could expect a very red scalp later that evening.

Aloe, Ow Are Ew?

I was always the kid you'd see swimming with a T-shirt on because I got sunburned so easily. On one occasion when I was ten years old, I went to a water park where shirts were not allowed on certain water slides. Finally sick of taking off and putting on a sopping wet shirt, I went without it for the rest of the day.

When I got home that evening, I was sunburned so badly that I was covered with blisters from my waist up. Trying to soothe my pain, I went to the medicine cabinet and pulled out some aloe vera gel to lather on my lobster red skin. I could barely stand the stinging sensation whenever I touched the aloe to my skin. Aloe was supposed to soothe the skin, not sting. I looked at the heap of green aloe gel in my hand and noticed little specks of sand in it. Apparently this bottle of aloe had made a trip to the beach where it had been dropped in the sand. I was actually rubbing a gel-like sandpaper all over my sunburned body.

Since the aloe was a no-go, my mom got her medical encyclopedia out and read that dabbing vinegar on sunburned skin would take away the sting. I ran to the pantry and grabbed the vinegar. I stood in the bathtub and poured every last drop of vinegar all over my body. That book was full of it! I still hurt all over, and now I smelled like I was fermenting. Oh, the humanity!

STAR-SPANGLED SHIRT

The ceremony began with the principal, Mr. Rosenquist, welcoming one and all to such a joyous event. He asked the crowd to stand, remove their hats, and join the choir in honoring our country with the national anthem.

Jolly Old Grecian

"To Anacreon in Heaven" was the drinking song of the Anacreontic Society, a club formed in honor of the Greek poet Anacreon. The tune was composed by a member of the society, John Stafford Smith, with lyrics by Ralph Tomlinson. The melody became famous after Francis Scott Key wrote "In Defense of Fort McHenry" while detained on a British ship during the War of 1812. Key set the poem to the society's tune, and it was later retitled "The Star-Spangled Banner" and officially became the U.S. national anthem in 1931.

One must wonder why the original lyrics did not evoke such patriotic emotion with phrases that included:

From that jolly old Grecian:
Voice, fiddle and flute no longer be mute,
I'll lend you my name and inspire you to boot.

Sounds like old Ralph Tomlinson must have knocked back one too many before setting his quill to the parchment.

I was part of that choir. It was the one class that I looked forward to regularly, not only because I enjoyed music and singing, but also because the altos and sopranos outnumbered the tenors and basses three to one.

My assigned part was first tenor, but truth be told, I could have sung soprano on most songs since my voice didn't change until I was almost fourteen.

All God's People Have a Place in the Choir

The voice change is the result of structural changes in the larynx, or voice box, under the influence of the male hormone testosterone. The specific age this takes place will depend on when puberty begins, and puberty may begin anytime between ages ten and fourteen. There is then a gradual change or deepening of the voice throughout puberty. The average age for completion of voice change is between fourteen and sixteen, but just as there is a significant variation in puberty, so is there in voice change. How low the voice goes depends on many factors, and it is not possible to give an exact answer. Some men are tenors (singing high), and others are basses (singing low).

As I belted out the tenor part of "The Star-Spangled Banner," I scanned the audience and saw a diamond glimmering in the sea of coal. It was Sunny Gersbach sitting in the third row between the Fs and Hs. She was looking at me, which was truly remarkable in itself, but she was also sort of smiling. Could I have looked so striking in my getup that I had finally caught the attention of Ms. Gersbach herself?

"And the rockets red glare," I sang with a newly found invigoration for a song I'd heard a thousand times.

"The bombs bursting in air…" Yep, she was still looking. Just to her right Nater Fallstream (why couldn't my last name have started with an *f* so I could sit next to Sunny?) began laughing and giving me a big thumbs-up. I couldn't tell if it was a "if I could only be as cool as Butterworth" thumbs-up or if it was more of a sarcastic "I know something you don't know" thumbs-up.

"Gave proof through the night…" What was he laughing at?

"That our flag was still there…" Confidence quickly turned to insecurity as I sweat in the summer sun.

"Oh say, does that star-spangled…" I began to panic and ran through a laundry list of possible things that could be spawning the laughter.

1. Am I singing the wrong words? No.
2. Is someone behind me giving me bunny ears? Hopefully not. That's not even funny, anyway. Who came up with the idea that flashing a peace sign above someone's head looked like bunny ears? And after that somewhat obvious realization, why did they think it was funny enough to carry on for generations?
3. Do I have spinach in my teeth? No. I hadn't eaten spinach since I gagged on it in the second grade.
4. Had he remembered something funny I had told him earlier? Doubtful.
5. Is my zipper down?

When I got to this point on my list, I looked down at my pants to check if the barn door was open, but when I gazed downward, I saw my shirt, and the question was suddenly answered. Apparently the mixture of hot sun, high temperatures, and thirty bodies packed onto two risers had been a lethal combo for my prepubescent sweat glands. Rayon was a bad choice.

The sweat had turned my shirt various shades of green, making it more army camouflage than stylish emerald. I looked like a GI Joe fighting off the evil powers of perspiration that sought to destroy the remaining dry spots on my shirt.

Proud parents roared as the choir belted out "the home of the brave!" Amid the applause we filed off according to our sections. Unfortunately, the tenors were the last to leave. I had hoped that Nater hadn't pointed out my mishap to Sunny. On this occasion her ignorance was my bliss. I scanned the audience to get a reassuring smile from my family but noticed quickly that I could find only my dad. He was easy to locate with his white blond hair, heavy-framed glasses, and proud grin.

Name: William Jesse Butterworth Jr.
Nickname: Bill or Dad
Stats: It took my dad forty years to move out of the decade he was born into. A regular Ward Cleaver, my dad had always been a man of convictions, a man of principles, and a man of ritual. Hair was to be cut neatly, dinner was to be served nightly, and church was to be attended weekly. In accordance with these midcentury principles, my dad also firmly believed that unruly children should be punished swiftly and that the father should pull the lion's share of the load in supporting and taking care of the family.

You need not search far to see where this behavior stemmed from. My dad was raised by a mother who served the same seven dishes each week for his entire upbringing and a father who fashioned one hair style his entire life and ate the same breakfast (cornflakes) every morning. His parents lacked the ability to communicate love and encouragement, which, in turn, made my dad the most loving and encouraging father on the face of this earth. For example, I could claim that by rubbing two sticks of chewing gum together I had discovered a new way to communicate with nonpoisonous jellyfish. Instead of pointing out the obvious absurdity of my claim, my dad would find some way to encourage my "imaginative innovation" or "out-of-the-box thinking."

A truly hilarious guy with a wit as sharp as a surgical knife, he was always teaching me the importance of comical timing and knowing your audience.

He was the guy I always looked up to, the guy I always wanted to be.

I found my dad in the crowd but noticed he was with my brothers Jeffrey and John and no one else.

Where's Mom? I thought.

I scanned the rest of the field frantically trying to find her. At last I saw her straight, sandy blond hair toward the back of the herd with the rest of my siblings.

Did they come separately to my graduation? I thought. *How lame is that?*

Name: *Rhonda Lynn Butterworth*
Nickname: **Mom**
Stats: Growing up was a frightening ordeal for my mom. She grew up in a small midwestern town where her parents

owned and operated a mom-and-pop restaurant called Dog and Suds. They were usually home only to sleep and left her to fend for herself in a big empty house that many people say was haunted. Rumor had it that the house was built by a Civil War general and his beloved wife. When his wife died suddenly, he couldn't stand the thought of being apart from her, so he buried her in the basement to keep her always near him. Every creak and crack in the house became a reminder of the general's wife, who haunted anyone who lived there. It's no wonder my mom was plagued by nightmares growing up.

It was always my mother's wish to marry, have six children, and live far away from her family. Fifteen hundred miles, five children, and three miscarriages later, my mom nearly got all that she wanted. But as you can imagine, raising five children while your husband is working overtime every week can wear down even the toughest individual. Finally, after seventeen years of putting her family first and her needs last, she had grown tired.

She homeschooled all of us kids until we reached junior high. She homeschooled us, not only to make sure that we got the one-on-one attention she thought we deserved, but also to make sure that we stayed kids as long as possible. When kids my age were learning bad words, looking at *Playboy* in the back of the bus, and being offered cigarettes, we were pretending to be Indiana Jones in our front yard, reading about the land of Narnia, and eating single slices of

American cheese. Her philosophy on learning is "the most important education is using your imagination."

She has quirky eating habits like taking the jelly out of her jelly doughnut and spreading it over the outside. Or if she eats bacon, eggs, and toast, she always cuts up the bacon and eggs, stirs them together, and scoops the mixture onto her toast. It's funny how I never knew these eating habits were strange until I went to college. I would eat my jelly doughnuts and bacon and eggs the same way she does, and my classmates would always ask me why I ate that way. "What way?" was usually my response. "You're telling me this isn't normal?"

Perhaps it wasn't the norm, but that's what I loved about it. And that's part of what I love about my mom.

The Other Side of the Platform

"William Jesse Butterworth the Third," the vice principal declared.

I walked up onto the stage, and thanks to the setting sun and the cooling temperatures, my shirt had returned to its original color. I shook Mr. Rosenquist's hand with my right hand and accepted the diploma with my left. I looked to my dad and then over to my mom. They were in the same place but seemed miles and miles away. Although it had not been verbalized at that point, my eighth-grade graduation not only marked the end of junior high. It also marked the end of an era in the Butterworth household. I knew our family would never be the same.

Stepping off that platform, I was aware that my life was about to change, but I had no idea just how much. Looking back now, I wouldn't mind returning to the other side of that platform. The festive family Christmas that would last for hours as we opened presents one by one. Having my mom help me with math homework and my dad help me with my English homework. Becoming the most celebrated person in the household when my birthday rolled around. Or having that subtle reassurance that my whole weird, dysfunctional family, whom I loved so much, was sleeping peacefully under the same roof. It was a place of comfort. A place of predictability. A place I could call home.

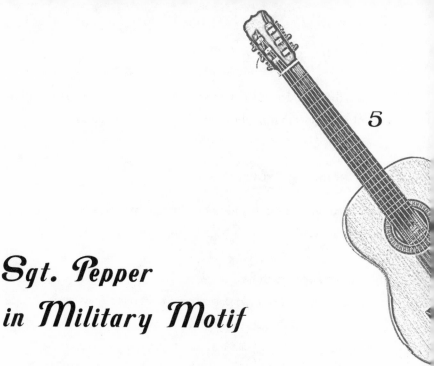

5

Sgt. Pepper in Military Motif

The summer between middle school and high school started off about as boring as it possibly could. Without a driver's license or any friends who could drive, I was left to rely on the Butterworth Taxi Company, whose two employees were getting sick of taxiing their five kids around. I didn't want to ask them for a ride anyway, because that raised the possibility of actually having to talk to them.

Like most kids that age, I had totally lost the ability and the desire to have a conversation with my parents. It was amazing how stupid they were. They had completely lost the ability to make any sense whatsoever. With every moronic utterance from their mouths, my eyes couldn't help but roll to the back of my head. (But don't worry. Dad and Mom eventually grew out of it. They got a lot smarter by the time I turned nineteen.)

One fateful July day I was avoiding my parents as usual and was completely bored out of my gourd. Looking for something, anything, to pass the time, I wandered into the garage. Perhaps there was a project of some sort that might pacify my tortured brilliance.

An Uncharted World

I checked out the wood and found enough materials for me to build another go-cart.

Inertia Will Hurtcha

The previous summer my mom had come home with a go-cart that she had found at a garage sale. Finally seeing the upside of having such a steep driveway, all the siblings took turns riding it down the driveway, where the rest of the siblings would help push it back up the hill. Not being ones to miss the fun, my mom and dad came out to give it a whirl. Mom whizzed down the driveway, screaming and laughing all the way. When Dad got his turn, there was screaming but very little laughter. His adult body dwarfed the go-cart as we gave him a nudge down the hill. Gravity immediately kicked in, and he was flying down the hill faster than any of us had gone. As Dad went around the bend, the plastic wheels on the outside of the cart could no longer handle the pressure and shattered into a thousand pieces, causing the go-cart to flip over several times in true NASCAR style. Unfortunately for my dad, he was still on it during its gymnastics routine. As we all ran to him in the cloud of dust, my sister asked, "Are you all right?"

He had survived with just a few bumps and bruises. Seeing there were no broken bones, I immediately went over to the go-cart and exclaimed, "Oh man! I can't believe you broke it!" How's that for loving compassion?

I had enough wood, but there were no wheels. I had already taken the wheels off the outside garbage can to replace the busted wheels on the go-cart. This was not a very smart move, because it made my chore of taking the garbage to the curb a royal pain.

I think I remember reading that a visionary completely ignores the obvious to achieve the spectacular. Hey, at least I had the first part down. Unfortunately, the wheels lasted for only a couple of runs before we witnessed a repeat of my dad's crash, except this time John was at the helm. After flipping over several times and taking the steering wheel in the face, he rose from the dust cloud, covered in dirt and blood and smiling like he wanted to do it again. Tough as nails, I tell ya.

I started taking cardboard boxes off the storage shelves looking for the four wheels that would complete my Frankenstein push-start-cart. I grabbed a box marked "Records."

The thought process of a mad genius/visionary such as myself is hard to chart and even harder to explain. I will try to break down my extremely complex thought process as simply as I can. Don't get too down on yourself if this elevated logic whizzes over your head.

Wheels are round.

Records are also round.

Perhaps if I use enough records, I could…

I know it is probably difficult to follow, but I can't waste any more time trying to explain the process of brilliance.

I ripped open the box to find an uncharted world, a new territory yet to be discovered: my dad's old record collection.

The go-cart idea was quickly shelved as I flipped through the cardboard sleeves and recognized some of the names: the Beatles; the Beach Boys; James Taylor; Paul Simon; Billy Joel; Elton John; Crosby, Stills, Nash and Young; Blood, Sweat, and Tears; Stevie Wonder.

Most of the cover pictures looked like a joke to me—the ridiculously outdated fashions, the shaggy hairdos, and the psychedelic artwork in paisley and pastel. This was clearly a far cry from the music that was hitting the airwaves at the time. Seattle grunge had invaded MTV (back when they actually showed music videos) with groups like Nirvana, Pearl Jam, Soundgarden, and Smashing Pumpkins. The underlying angst in the music was something I could connect with; however, I wasn't really crazy about the music itself. It seemed like a bunch of depressed dudes in flannel shirts and Doc Martens, singing about how hard their lives were or at least how hard they had made them. I got what they were saying, but I put my headphones on for an escape, not complexity. I have plenty of complexity already.

I schlepped the heavy box into my bedroom and took the records out one at a time. Although the people on the covers looked like they were from a distant time and place, something in their eyes resonated with me. It was a look of pleasure and pain, reality and fantasy, loathing and love—all lurking beneath the surface. It was beckoning me to listen.

I went back out to the garage and found our old family hi-fi (that's old-people talk for record player) and put it on top of my stereo in my bedroom. I was missing the wire to hook up the hi-fi to my stereo, so I ended up jerry-rigging something.

Jerry-rig

That Jerry guy must have been one innovative dude, always using what he could find to rig things to work. And what about that Josh guy? Must have been a real kidder if he was always "Joshin" people. Or the world's worst golfer, Mulligan, famous for his do overs. And then there was Scott, always getting off so free. Of course there's that Alec fella whose sarcasm became known as "smart." And then there's Murphy. Was he just the most unlucky man alive to have that law named after him?

Thank you. I'll be here all weekend. Don't forget to tip your waitress.

With the hi-fi finally hooked up, I grabbed a record by a group called Sly and the Family Stone and set it on the turntable. With anticipation brewing and the black circle spinning, I grabbed the arm and gently placed the needle on the edge of the record.

Instead of the much-anticipated music, a horrible scratching sound came out of the speakers, and I quickly lifted the arm from the record. Apparently, during its years on the garage shelf, the hi-fi had never received a replacement needle after the old one had broken.

Puff Daddy Warbucks

The last needle fell victim to my brother Jeffrey. We loved to listen to the soundtrack of the movie *Annie* when we were younger, and we were less than delicate with the record. After several months of abuse at the hands of my siblings, the record skipped so much that it sounded more like an *Annie* remix by Puff Daddy Warbucks. Jeffrey thought the problem was not the actual record but the needle, so he grabbed a dishtowel and scrubbed the needle until it just popped right off.

I was so intent on getting the record player up and working so I could unlock the mystery of the vinyl unknown that I was willing to take desperate measures. "Dad," I said, "can you take me to Radio Shack?"

With a surprised expression, my dad looked up from the Dodgers game.

We Put the Jumbo in JumboTron

At the last Dodger game we attended, my sister and brothers and I made it our goal to be put on the JumboTron. Once we hit the eighth inning, we noticed that the cameramen were getting closeups of kids who had fallen asleep in their seats. Seeing our golden opportunity, we all put our heads on each other's shoulders and pretended we were sleeping peacefully in hopes that the camera operator would make our JumboTron dreams a reality. Alas, after two innings of faking sleep, we finally gave up and stuffed our faces with Dodger dogs.

I don't think it was the question that baffled my dad but rather the eight unprovoked words that came out of my mouth.

"What for?" he asked.

"I want to get a new needle for the hi-fi," I replied.

I couldn't read the expression on his face. For fear of getting in trouble for not asking first, I didn't want to tell him I had already brought all his old records inside.

"Did you find my old records?"

Shoot. How did he know? "Yeah," I said, uncertain of the consequences.

"Mmmmm." He paused, stood, and felt the contents of his pockets. "Let me grab my keys, and I'll meet you at the car."

DRUGS, BEATLES, AND RECORD NEEDLES

We hopped into my dad's retro, baby blue Mercedes and headed into town.

Give Me a Brake...Seriously

Remarkably my father has never been in an accident. He is infamous for following cars too closely and coming to sudden, unexpected stops. When he's driving and I'm sitting in the front seat, I spend most of the time grabbing the handle above the window and pressing the floor panel with my right foot, wishing there were a brake pedal. I'm sure you've ridden with someone like that.

"Now, you know you have to be very careful with those records," my dad explained.

"Yeah, I know." My eyes rolled.

"You can't throw them around like Frisbees. They're really fragile, and you have to be respectful of them." I couldn't tell if he was trying to say something about the way parents should be treated or the way records should be treated. Probably both.

"I know, Dad," I said in my most annoyed tone.

Seeing that he was breaking no new ground in this matter, we went back to our silence.

He reached over to the radio tuner and turned on Oldies 101. The Beatles classic "Lucy in the Sky with Diamonds" was playing.

"Do you know which Beatles album this is on?" he asked me.

"No," I said.

"It's on *Sgt. Pepper's Lonely Hearts Club Band,*" he answered. "I have this record at home. You probably noticed it when you were looking through the records. It has a very famous album cover."

"What does it look like?" I asked. My interest had been piqued because the album covers were still fresh in my mind.

"The Beatles are all dressed in old British military motif, and they're standing in front of a crowd of life-size cardboard cutouts of famous people."

"Oh yeah!" The connection had been made in my mind. "I've seen that one in there. I think I remember seeing a big poster for that when we were in San Francisco on a school field trip."

Poo-Poo Platter

On that same field trip to San Francisco, we took a ferry ride across the bay. The ferry offered hot clam chowder in sourdough bread bowls that were to die for. Above the ferry, a dozen begging sea gulls squawked for pieces of bread. Nater grabbed a piece of his bread bowl and launched it into the sky. Instantly, several sea gulls went right in to catch the bread in midair. Three of them caught it at the same time and ripped it in three, each gobbling its portion. As soon as the other students saw how cool this was, they all started grabbing portions of their bread bowls and tossing them into the air. Within seconds the twelve sea gulls multiplied into over one hundred, and a feeding frenzy ensued.

The unexpected spectacle above us was quite a hit with all the students on the boat. We all looked up, laughing and gawking at the whirling birds above. With no warning and no umbrellas, the cloud of feathers above us began to rain down. It initially looked like snow or hail, but this definitely was neither. As if the birds had strategized a bombing, the sky opened up and pooped on us. The crowded decks quickly emptied as the splattered people ran for cover. With the deck empty, it was easy to see all the signs posted around that clearly said Do Not Feed the Birds.

"Yeah, that's the album cover," he said with obvious excitement in his voice. "Anyway, this song is from the *Sgt. Pepper* album. Do you know what this song is about?"

"About a girl named Lucy?" I answered hopefully.

"Well, sort of. A lot of people think this song is about drugs."

"Why?" I asked.

"Well, do you know what LSD is?" he asked.

"Ummm…" Of course I knew what LSD was, but I didn't want to answer the question too quickly for fear he'd think I hung out with a bunch of druggies.

Sensing my hesitation, he went on. "LSD is a psychedelic drug that got very popular in the sixties, when this song was written. A lot of people thought that 'Lucy in the Sky with Diamonds' stood for LSD."

"But it didn't?" I asked.

"No." he said. "The name of the song came from John Lennon's son Julian, who had drawn a picture for him. When John asked his son what the picture was called, Julian replied, 'It's called "Lucy in the Sky with Diamonds."' John thought that was so clever that he ended up writing a song based on the picture his son drew."

"Interesting," I said.

I listened to the rest of the song with a new awareness. Of course it made even less sense to me as I really tried to home in on the words, but at least I knew it wasn't about drugs.

We pulled up to Radio Shack, and I was amazed by how quickly the usually much-dreaded car ride with my dad had gone. He continued telling me stories about the Beatles and the albums that filled the box at home.

We walked into the store, grabbed the needle for the record player, paid for it, and headed back home. Fortunately for us, Oldies 101 was having an all-Beatles weekend, so we rolled down the windows, put our hands in the wind, and turned up "Can't Buy Me Love" as loud as the old car radio could go.

I glanced over at my dad and had a revolutionary thought: *Maybe he's not as big an idiot as I've thought.*

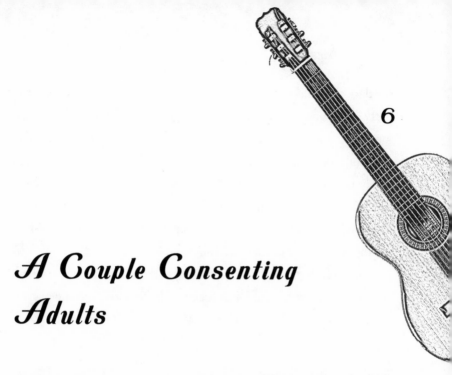

6

A Couple Consenting Adults

The following summer months just got worse and worse in the Butterworth household. The heat had become almost unbearable, and any activity that wasn't air-conditioned was not an option. The hotter the temperature got outside, the worse the fighting became inside.

Down the hall and behind closed doors, my mom and dad would have it out about God knows what on a daily basis. We could never fully decipher their words, but their screaming and shouting could be heard in every room in the house.

Joy had turned sixteen that summer and gotten her license and the old family car. Now mobile, she often visited friends to escape the fighting. My brothers would hang out at the house of a neighbor kid, Adam, where they would eat cheesy chips and play Nintendo all day. I, on the other hand, would escape into my bedroom, where a box of vinyl records gave me the distraction I longed for. I would barricade my door shut and spin those old records all day long, only leaving for potty breaks and mealtimes. I could get so lost in the music that sometimes an entire evening went by without my cracking open the door for food, water, or human contact.

In that room I would go to Carolina in my mind with James Taylor and cry for help right along with the Beatles. In the distance I could hear the train that Paul Simon was singing about, or I'd join in singing "la de da, la de da" with the Piano Man, Billy Joel. I knew the loneliness of Elton John's "Rocket Man" and felt that the Beach Boys' "In My Room" was written just for me. My bedroom was the place I could hide out and forget about the world crumbling around me.

The Family Meeting

There was a knock on my door, and my sister poked her head inside. "Mom and Dad want to have a family meeting in the family room in five minutes."

"Oh great," I said. "What for?"

"Dunno," she replied, "but I doubt it's good."

I shut off the record that was playing, got up from my desk, and went into the kitchen to get a drink of water. My two youngest brothers were there eating granola bars and talking.

"The first thing I'll do when we get to Disneyland is go on that new ride, Splash Mountain," John said to Joseph. "Adam said that you drop like a million miles per hour, and then you get all wet 'cause the water comes into the boat, and you totally get soaked."

"When are you going to Disneyland?" I asked.

"We're all going to Disneyland," he said.

"What?" I asked.

"Yeah, that's always what happens at family meetings. Dad and Mom tell us that we're all going on a trip to Disneyland," John said with Joseph looking very excited at every mention of it.

I couldn't argue with his logic. It was true. When we were called together for a family meeting, it usually meant we were going on a little vacation to Disneyland, but I didn't think that would be happening this summer.

"Well, we'll see," I said. "Try not to get your hopes up, though. Come on. Let's go."

The time had arrived, and all five of us kids sat in the family room when my mom and dad came in trying to mask the defeated look in their red, puffy eyes. John and Joseph looked like they could barely contain their excitement, Jeffrey just sat there staring straight ahead, and Joy already had tears in her eyes even before any words were spoken.

"Well," my mom started, searching for any words that might easily kick off this meeting. She wore a painted-on smile as she tried to keep a happy appearance. "Your dad and I want to tell you all that we're…" John and Joseph leaned forward in anticipation. "Well," she continued, "we've decided to split up for a little while." You could hear the air being sucked out of the room. John and Joseph looked thoroughly dazed and confused, and Jeffrey and Joy buried their faces in their hands. My stomach dropped to my ankles, and the burning in my eyes and throat couldn't be subdued. Without warning I found myself sobbing like a baby.

"We're not getting a divorce," my mom added, trying to include some tiny element of hope in this bombshell. "Your dad and I just need a little space from each other right now, so we're going to try this out for a month or so and see how it works."

A month or so, my butt, I thought.

Dad was sitting across from Mom, and both were trying their best to stay strong in their lowest moment, the moment that broke their children's hearts.

"The good news is," my mom continued, "that your dad will be less than a mile away in the apartment complex on the hill where there are tennis courts and a hot tub. He will have lots of videos you guys can watch if you get bored. You can have sleepovers there and visit him whenever you want."

I couldn't believe she had the audacity to try to put a positive spin on their splitting up. The very last things we kids were thinking about at the time was tennis, hot tubs, and sleepovers.

"I'm...I'm sorry, guys." My dad's voice cracked as he said this, as did the dam that had been holding back his tears. He completely lost it and began to weep openly. At this sight, everyone, including my mom, became a blubbering mess. We all sat there in the family room weeping.

I wiped the tears from my eyes and looked around at us, a broken family. The younger boys, Joseph and John, were crying, not only because of the news, but also out of confusion and utter disappointment that we weren't going to Disneyland. I could see the chip on Jeffrey's shoulder getting bigger and bigger, and I could hear Joy's fragile spirit break into a thousand tiny pieces. And then I looked at my parents, both weeping and walking toward us kids with open arms. I couldn't stomach the thought of hugging my parents, so I got up and bolted into my room. I slammed the door and buried my head in my pillow and cried until I was heaving for air.

WHO'S AT FAULT?

It wasn't like the announcement of the split was a total surprise, but it's like when you find out your grandma has Alzheimer's disease. You're not sure exactly how to deal with it. You know that she's not dead, because you can still see her living and breathing, but you can't help feeling like she really is dead. Is it worth sitting and talking to her when you're not really sure she's hearing you? Is it worth giving her a hug when you're not sure she has any clue who you are? You can't figure out if it's easier to act like she's still alive or act like she's passed away. And when you finally hear that she's breathed her last breath, all the emotions you've held in limbo come gushing out, and you can't do anything to stop it.

When you have such deep feelings of anguish over something that's been lost, a natural reaction is "Who did this?" or "Whose fault is this?" Which, in turn, leads to thoughts of revenge or retribution.

I'd heard people say on after-school specials, "It's not your fault that your parents are divorcing." I couldn't agree more. There are probably a lot of kids who feel that something they did or didn't do caused their folks to split. To them I offer that same after-school-special advice: *it's not your fault.* In my case, however, it never crossed my mind that I had caused the breakup. I knew it was my parents' fault.

Take T-bone, for example. When I made fun of T-bone on the blacktop, he first had feelings of total anguish and may have thought, *If only I were thin.* But after he realized he didn't deserve to take that kind of stuff, he immediately sought out the one who had made it happen.

In the case of my parents' splitting up, it was difficult to pick out who had caused this, and as far as I could tell, they were both the good guys and both the bad guys.

Speaking with the Enemy

There was a knock, and Mom opened my door and came in and sat on the foot of my bed.

"How are you doing?" she asked.

"How do you think?" I said.

"Well, I'm not sure," she said.

"I feel like %#*, okay?" I was so enraged I didn't even pause for her to react to my blatant act of defiance. "First of all, I can't believe you guys are going through with actually splitting up, and, second, I can't believe you were trying to put a happy face on this whole thing. Woo hoo, hot tubs!" I said in my most sarcastic tone. "Tennis courts! Sleepovers! Well, I'd rather have my parents under the same roof."

We sat in silence for a few seconds while I completely avoided any eye contact with my mother.

"I know, honey," she finally said, "but...it's for the best." She gave my leg a reassuring squeeze and then got up and left the room.

I watched my mom leave and had these strange, complex feelings of loving her and hating her all in the same moment.

One Huge Favor

Later that afternoon my dad came with a moving truck. It was obvious that this move had been some time in the making. The apartment was already rented, the moving truck had been reserved, my dad's office had been mostly boxed up, and his clothes had been packed— all unbeknown to us.

We gathered around the truck to give my dad a hand in loading it.

"Listen," he said, "I know that this whole day has been really,

really hard on all of you, and it's been really, really hard on your mother and me as well. I just want you to know that we love you all more than ever, and I would love to have you guys come over anytime you want to." Our chins quivered at the thought of not having our dad around all the time.

"I also need to ask you one huge favor. I need you guys to keep this a secret for a while until I'm able to personally tell all of my clients so they don't hear it from somebody else." I hadn't thought about that. My dad's profession was speaking and writing about family values, and now he was splitting with his wife. It was the final nail in the coffin of his career. What would he do now?

Divorce leaves no victims unscathed.

MY FATHER'S SCENT

We started carrying his stuff out to the truck and loaded it carefully. The sick feeling in the pit of my stomach increased with every cardboard box we stacked. My father's scent wafted through the dusty truck full of his belongings. I would deeply miss that smell.

"What are you guys doing? Are you moving?" Being so wrapped up in the emotion of packing my dad's stuff, we had failed to notice Adam, the neighbor kid, standing near the back of the truck.

"Ummm…" I could see the wheels in John's head spinning quickly. "Well, ummm, my dad's moving to a new office." Both he and Adam looked satisfied with this explanation until my dad and Jeffrey came around the corner lugging a mattress.

"Then why is he taking a mattress?" Adam asked inquisitively.

"Well…" John looked panicked. "We've got tons of mattresses, and we don't really need them all here at the house, so…"

I couldn't bear to see my brother back-pedal like this, so I stepped in.

"Look, Adam, it's time for you to go home," I said to a surprised Adam.

"Oh, okay," he said.

"John and Joseph will come over when they're ready to play, okay?"

"Okay," he replied and was on his way back down the steep driveway. The same driveway where my dad crashed that go-cart or would honk the tune to "shave and a haircut" every time he came home from a business trip. The same driveway he would soon be leaving on.

Life would never be the same again.

7

I Just Had to Get Away

The next few weeks inched by slowly. My dad's absence from the home left a huge hole, and I missed him deeply. I had walked over to his place a few times, but the summer heat, my naturally lazy nature, and my complicated feelings of love and resentment toward my parents kept me from getting there more often. And truth be told, even if I could have gotten there more, I don't know that I would have gone. My dad had fallen into a deep, dark depression that he tried to hide, but it was like trying to hide an oil spill with a white sheet. It always showed through.

I continued to lock myself in my room and lose myself in music but found that I had acquired an insatiable taste for more than just sitting back and listening. I wanted to become an active participant, not just in the music, but also in my life. I had so many emotions completely pent up inside that were trying to surface, but I was too young and immature to know how to work through my feelings in a healthy and productive way. I started to seek out different ways to express myself. I decided I wanted to be a rebel.

I had noticed an obvious change in my brother Jeffrey over the past couple of months. He was completely ignoring my mom and had never gone to visit my dad. He was a mad little man looking for an outlet for all his anger. He started hanging out with the hard-core kids, and it quickly became known that he was not someone to mess with. I understood his frustration but was not nearly as hard-core as he was.

Warrior Poet

Years later when Jeffrey was in high school, he trained to be a boxer. He was in perfect shape and had a shaved head, black army boots, and a look of animosity in his eye. Even the neo-Nazis knew not to mess with Jeffrey Butterworth. He could take down just about any-body who got in his path, but the biggest battle he ever had to fight was how to reconcile with Mom and Dad. Nowadays he's the nicest, gentlest guy you'd ever meet, but deep in his heart there's a warrior poet with battle scars galore.

Being a pretty good kid most of my life, I thought that being a rebel meant sneaking Ritz crackers when my mom had said, "No snacks before dinner." When it came to mutiny, I was a real light-weight, but I decided I was going to show the world that I was sick of my life and wasn't going to take it anymore.

I picked up the phone and dialed Aaron's number.

"Hey," I said when he answered, "do you think your brother can give us a ride somewhere tonight?"

"Where are we going?" he asked.

I cleared my throat and in my best tough-guy voice said, "We're gonna do a bad, bad thing."

ON DA VIC

Aaron's older brother, Ryan, rolled into my driveway in his tiny, light blue Honda Civic hatchback. Inspired by the clever Toyota truck owners who would paint over the letters OTA so the tailgate read TOY, Ryan had taken a razor blade to the letters of his car so that it read "ON DA VIC." It made absolutely no sense to anyone else, but Ryan thought it was funnier than passing gas in church. Suffice it to say, Ryan was not the sharpest knife in the drawer.

I walked out to the driveway as he pulled in. Aaron was sitting in the passenger seat and waved when he saw me. Ryan parked, got out of the car, and pushed the driver's seat forward. From the back of the compact car, T-bone, Stick, and Nater all emerged like clowns from a tiny VW.

"What the flip are you guys doing here?" I asked the gang after they squeezed out of the car.

"And hello to you, too," Nater replied.

"How did you know..."

T-bone interrupted me before I could finish. "Aaron called and said we were going to do something cool. So what is it?"

"Ummm, well...let's get in the car, and I'll tell you on the way."

As the God Squad piled back into Ryan's tiny car, I remembered something I needed to grab.

"I'll be back in a sec, guys," I said as I ducked into the dark garage. I flipped the light switch and was quickly reminded that the bulb had burned out. I felt around the workbench and grabbed the only saw I could find. I stumbled around as I felt my way back out-side. When I opened the back of Ryan's car to throw the saw in, I was assaulted by the smells of melted crayons and fast-food grease. I slammed the hatchback closed and opened the passenger-side door.

"Okay," Ryan asked, "where are we going?"

"Head toward the river," I replied as I shoved myself in the tiny backseat with three others.

"Are we going skinny-dipping?" T-bone asked apprehensively, no doubt not looking forward to shedding his shirt in front of his peers.

"No," I said, "we're going to steal ourselves a street sign."

There was a collective "whoa" as the gang looked at each other, wondering what they'd gotten themselves into.

"Why don't we just mess with the L.O.P. sign like everybody else does?" Aaron asked.

Lake of the What?

There was a gated community about a mile from our school called Lake of the Pines or, more commonly, L.O.P. The popular thing to do was for someone to act as a decoy and blow through the gated area in his car so that the guard on duty had to leave his post and chase after the culprit. Meanwhile, when the guard was gone, another group of kids unscrewed the letters on the giant sign at the entrance. They would switch the letters i and e of the word *Pines* so that the sign said something very different. The next morning when the school buses passed by, there would be a collective snicker.

"Because everybody does that, and it's barely considered illegal," I said. "Stealing a street sign is way more dangerous."

"Why are we stealing a street sign?" Stick asked, breaking his silence to ask the obvious question.

"Because we need to, Stick." I tried to sound as authoritative as a slightly insecure twelve-year-old could. "We need to send a message to the world that it's time we start calling our own shots. Now, are you in or are you out?"

"Yeah, okay," Stick replied.

"All right then, let's do this," I said as we drove through the summer night toward the river.

MAYBE IT'S A SIGN

After twenty minutes of being smushed like sardines in the backseat, we finally arrived at our destination.

"Just park the car here, Ryan," I instructed.

We all flopped out of the car and stretched.

"There it is, boys." I pointed to the street sign that stood proudly in front of us, warning people of curves that can be slippery when wet and of the speed limit of fifteen miles per hour. She was a giant beauty, backlighted by the full moon and towering over us in splendor.

"How the heck are we going to get that home?" Nater asked as the river trickled behind him.

"Simple," I said as I pulled the saw out of the back of the car. "We cut it down."

"Are you serious?" Aaron asked.

"Yeah, that wood is thick," Nater said. "It would take us forever."

"Don't worry. We'll just switch off sawing until it's cut through," I said trying to rally the troops.

"Ummm…" Stick was tapping my shoulder.

"What?" I said as I turned around.

"That saw is for cutting metal pipes, not wood," he said.

"What are you talking about?" But before I could finish my thought, I looked down at the saw, and moonlight reflected a hacksaw, not the wood saw I had intended to grab.

"Well," T-bone said, "guess we better head home."

"No way. We're gonna do this thing right now!" I knelt at the base of the sign and began sawing with every angry fiber within me.

"You'll never get through that thing," Nater said.

"Watch me," I said defiantly, sawing vehemently. However, my anger fueled me for only about a minute, and then I needed a break. "Okay, who's up next?" I asked.

No one said a word.

"Come on, guys, are you in or are you out?" This had worked for me in the car earlier, and I was hoping it would work again.

"All right," Aaron said as he stepped up and grabbed the saw. "We're going straight to hell in a head gasket."*

---

*Correct saying: Going to hell in a handbasket

Definition: To deteriorate rapidly without any effort

It's Auto This World!

Waldo Kent, Ryan and Aaron's late grandpa, owned the finest mechanic's shop in town—Auto This World. Of course Waldo was married to Aaron's grandma Eileen for thirty-some years, and the habit of messing up old sayings rubbed off on Waldo as well as

Aaron. So between Eileen and Auto This World, Waldo concocted the saying "to hell in a head gasket."

As Aaron leaned down to saw, T-bone noticed headlights coming our way. "Someone's coming! Quick, hide!" T-bone shouted.

We all dived for cover under the trees and shrubs on the side of the road. The car whizzed by, completely ignoring the speed limit. We all got up and wiped ourselves off.

"That was a close one," Ryan said.

"All right," I said, "no harm, no foul. Let's do this thing."

Aaron continued sawing until he was spent. "Who's next?" he asked.

We gathered around to see how much farther there was to go.

"We'll never get this thing down," Nater said.

"Come on. Let's just go home," Aaron said.

I couldn't believe it. Even my rebellion was going wrong. Nothing seemed to be going right in my life. I became so angry just thinking about it that I started a full-on run at the sign, screaming as I ran.

"Jesse!" the guys yelled in the background, trying to stop me.

I hit the sign straight on with my shoulder and was knocked over on my side. I hit the ground, heaving for air, but I could hear all the guys oohing and aahing. I looked up. The sign was tilted.

"Look what you did, dude," Aaron said.

"The ground is soft because we're by the river," Stick informed us.

"Come on," I said. "Help me." We began rocking the sign back and forth until it finally came free of the ground. "We did it!" I exclaimed as the guys let out a mighty cry of victory. "Now let's load this bad boy up."

Like hunters celebrating their kill, we gathered around the sign and picked it up. Ryan opened the hatchback of his tiny car, and we loaded the sign. Of course we had not completely thought through this part of the plan. The sign with post was nearly eight feet long and had a ball of concrete at the bottom. We were able to shove only about five feet of the sign into the car, so we had three feet of wood with a concrete ball hanging out the back.

"Someone's coming!" T-bone shouted as headlights headed our way.

"Quick, get in!" I yelled.

We piled into the car as Ryan started the engine. Sitting in the already too crowded backseat with a giant street sign overhead was not so comfortable.

"Go, go, go!" Aaron shouted as the headlights came closer.

"I'm trying," Ryan said. "I can't get it to move."

"Duck!" T-bone yelled as the car sped past us. I'm not sure what the logic was in ducking since the sign was totally visible and a cement glob was hanging out the back of the car, but we felt good about hiding.

"Okay, let's go," I implored Ryan when the coast was clear.

"I can't!" he said. "That's what I was trying to tell you. This car won't budge an inch."

Aaron got out of the passenger seat to see if there was some kind of problem. He circled around the back of the car and discovered that the wheel wells were resting on the tires.

"There's no way this thing is going to go with all of us *and* the sign," Aaron announced.

"Fine," I said trying to think quickly. "T-bone, Nater, Stick—you guys wait here while we take the sign back to my house, and then we'll come back and get you."

"Yeah, right," Nater said. "My curfew is in less than an hour."

"Mine, too," T-bone said.

"Well that's just perfect!" I said. "So what the heck are we going to do with this street sign?"

"Put it back," Stick replied.

Although I hated to admit it, Stick was right. There was nothing left to do but put the sign back where we'd found it. We picked up the sign and carried it back to its resting place like pallbearers hauling a casket. We set it in the ground, packed the dirt around it, and just stood there and stared at it.

"Car!" Ryan cried out. "Duck!"

We all jumped down the river's bank like before, hoping not to be spotted by the oncoming car. Then I realized that an outsider would see nothing wrong, and therefore we had no reason to hide.

"Get up, you guys," I said. "We have no reason to hide anymore."

We stood up, brushed ourselves off, and crammed back into Ryan's car to head home. It was a long ride.

A Mad
Little Man

T he morning after the failed attempt to steal the street sign, there was an overall feeling among the God Squad that we should attend church. So Ryan swung by everybody's house and gave us a ride to church in his ON DA VIC. We sat through some seriously ear-bending music by Jeremy Milky, a high-school sophomore who led our times of worship.

The Milky Way

Jeremy Milky was infamous for taking popular songs on the radio and changing the words so they would have some kind of Christian connotation. For example, he tried to redeem the words to "I Wanna Sex You Up" by changing them to "I Want to Lift You Up" and "Smells Like Teen Spirit" to "Smells Like Holy Spirit." Mostly these songs just brought waves of laughter in the youth group instead of the unbridled praise I'm sure Jeremy had originally intended. Although it was completely ludicrous, you can't fault the guy for trying.

We were sitting in the row where we always parked our rears as Art, the youth pastor, began his talk. Art was the kind of guy you never took too seriously. He desperately tried to keep his hand on the pulse of what kids were doing so as not to appear irrelevant or dorky. However, a middle-aged guy who talks and dresses like a junior higher should always be viewed as a Proceed with Caution sign.

When it came to Sunday morning topics, Art generally spoke on four subjects in rotation:

1. Don't have sex. (That would mean I'd have to have a girl stand within ten feet of me. Wasn't going to happen.)

2. Don't drink or do drugs. (I can't stand the taste of alcohol and wouldn't have the foggiest idea where to get drugs even if I were interested in taking them. Wasn't going to happen either.)

3. Don't worship idols. (Art never did a really good job of expounding on what modern-day idols might look like, so we thought he was talking about the kind of idols in the Old Testament. There was not a chance I would be worshiping statues, mannequins, or totem poles anytime soon, so that definitely was not going to happen either.)

4. Honor your father and mother. (*Oh crud.* No comment.)

Of course, honor your father and mother was the topic of choice on that particular Sunday morning. I squirmed in my chair as Art tried to unpack the meaning of this commandment for a group of junior highers who viewed their parents as a species of lower intellect. I don't remember much of what he said, but every time he repeated the phrase "honor your father and mother," my stomach got a little tighter and my anger a little hotter. Clearly, Art's parents had never divorced or completely let him down! How could he even begin to understand what I was going through when he was up there wearing his neon-colored parachute pants, his Oakley sunglasses pushed on top of his head, and his Nike shoes that have a pump for a tongue—and waving a Bible and acting like he knew what he was talking about? Ohhh, and now he was bringing God into it.

"God knows how you're feeling," he said. "God knows it's hard to honor your parents sometimes. God knows what you're going through."

At this statement I couldn't take it anymore. I stood up and left under the guise of having to use the bathroom, then roamed the hallways, stewing in my anger until church was finally over and I could get a ride home.

If God understands what I'm going through, then why doesn't He do something about it? I thought as I walked the halls. *If He's so loving and kind and whatever, why isn't He loving or kind to me?*

As I was roaming, I walked past the worship center where the normal nine o'clock service was almost over. The back doors of the room were open, and I could see the congregation standing and singing "How Great Thou Art."

"How great Thou art—*right!*" I muttered to myself. "Clearly God doesn't give a rip."

Skunk You

Ryan's overloaded car barely made it up the steep driveway to my house, but we all leaned forward hoping to help the car up the hill. Once we finally reached the top, I hopped out and marched into the house and straight to my room, still stewing in the frustrations of the morning.

"Jesse?" my mom yelled from the kitchen.

"What?" I answered sharply.

"This is the third time I've asked you to take out the trash," she yelled.

"Whatever!" I responded.

"Jesse!" My door flew open, and my mom's head appeared. "Take out the trash right now!"

"Why don't you do it?" I said defiantly. She had picked the wrong morning to mess with me.

"Excuse me?" she said, obviously giving me the chance to correct myself.

"I said why don't you go and do it yourself!" It felt good to say it.

"Jesse, get out here this instant and take the trash out!"

"No!" I shouted. "Skunk you!" The anger raged so hard through my body that the only thing I could think to do was shout, "Skunk you!" (I didn't really say "skunk," by the way. I'll let you imagine what I really said.)

The fire in my mother's eyes burned like a thousand suns.

"Get out here and take the trash out and then get right back in your room, because you are grounded, young man!" she retorted.

"You can't do that!" I was cussing like a sailor, but I couldn't stop myself. "I'm leaving! I'm getting out of here! I hate you!"

My mom briefly disappeared into the kitchen and returned with a roll of trash bags. My first thought was that she was really sticking to her guns on the whole take-the-trash-out thing, but she took out a bag, opened one of my dresser drawers, and dumped all of its contents into the trash bag.

"What are you doing?" I shouted.

"You're right," she said. "You are leaving. You're going to go live with your father."

She continued to empty the contents of my drawers into the trash bags.

"You can't do that!" I shouted.

"Watch me," she said as she dumped the contents of yet another drawer into a new trash bag.

"Skunk you!" I shouted as I bolted for the door. I ran outside and down the driveway. I was trying so hard to hold back the tears that I could barely breathe. I really wished I were the Flash at this point so I could run as far away as possible. I didn't know where I was going, but I knew I couldn't stay there. I ran down a few more streets and found a patch of manzanita trees I could hide under. I could no longer hold back the tears, and I began to weep hard and angrily.

"Why, God?" was all I could think to say at that moment of total brokenness. "Why, God?" I repeated over and over as I cried. I waited for an answer.

Half and Half

My relationship with God until this point had been fairly distant. Half of the time my feelings could best be described as a love you have for relatives you see only once a year. And the only time you really think about them is when they send you a gift or a check.

The other half of the time I felt like God was the policeman in the sky, watching every little thing I did wrong and waiting to bust me on it. The few times I voluntarily prayed consisted mostly of confession and asking for things.

Lying there under the manzanitas, I really did want to give God a chance to explain why He would let this happen. Why would He let a happy family break into a million tiny pieces and not do anything to stop it or help put it back together? I lay in silence, with the only sound being my heavy breathing mixed with the breeze blowing through the trees, but God didn't answer.

"Fine. You're silent. Then I'll be silent too." That was the last prayer I prayed for four years.

Don't Get Mad; Get Glad

When I finally calmed down, I tried to figure out where I would go. If I went home, my mom would certainly take me straight to my dad's apartment. And as far as I was concerned, I wanted to steer clear of my mom as long as I possibly could. None of my friends lived within walking distance, so the only logical place to go was my dad's apartment.

When I arrived at his place, his doorstep was piled high with white trash bags and cardboard boxes full of my stuff. I moved a couple of bags, found the doorbell, and rang it. Trash bags caved in on him like an avalanche as he opened the door. After the initial shock of dodging the avalanche, my dad looked up and saw his eldest son, his namesake, barely able to stand, with puffy eyes and a broken heart.

"Where have you been?" he asked.

"Mom kicked me out of the house." My voice cracked as I tried to explain.

"Yeah, I know," he said. "She called me. What did you do?"

"I cussed her out," I said staring at the ground.

"No, I mean what did you do after that?" he asked.

"I just ran away because I hate her!" I said.

"No you don't," he said in a comforting tone. "Come on in. I'm making some sandwiches for lunch." He grabbed a couple of trash bags to clear a path for my entry and put his arm around me. "The extra room's all ready for you to take over."

"Okay," I said.

CARRY THAT WEIGHT

I walked inside the apartment, and although it was still light outside, it was very dark inside. All the shades were drawn, and the only light came from the Dodgers' game on TV and a single lamp standing in the corner.

My dad was still fighting a deep depression, and I realized later that any time spent outside of that apartment was a major triumph for him. It became clear in a matter of weeks that no church wanted my dad to speak there when he was going through a divorce. I couldn't blame them for that, but what really made me sick—and does even to this day—was how many people completely turned their backs on both my mom and my dad. It was as if they didn't even exist anymore. I guess it's human nature to put people on pedestals, and when they come tumbling down for whatever reason, we don't want to see them bloodied and broken. We just want our pedestal person back. Right then both my mom and dad were definitely bloodied and broken and looking for support anywhere they could find it.

Dad's career had come to a grinding halt, and he had holed up in that apartment, waiting for the storm to pass. He left the apartment only once a day to go to the grocery store or to the post office to get his mail. With his career all but over and the paychecks not coming in, my dad was living like a college bachelor: pb&j, Cup o' Noodles, and laundry at the Laundromat.

"Here you go, buddy," he said as he handed me a sandwich.

"Thanks," I said, and we both sat in silence watching the rest of the Dodgers' game.

After the game was over, my dad helped me get my stuff into my new room. The first thing we did was set up the stereo and record player.

"You still listening to these old records?" my dad asked me.

"Yeah," I said, "all the time."

"Which one's your favorite?" he asked.

"I don't know," I replied, trying to narrow it down to at least my top five. "It's hard to say. There are too many."

"What have you been listening to lately?" he asked as he flipped through records he had acquired in his youth.

"I've been really into the Beatles' *Abbey Road* lately," I said.

"Yeah," he said smiling, "that's one of my favorites."

He kept looking through the records until he found the album and put it on the turntable. We both sang every word on that album as we unpacked my boxes and garbage bags. "Once there was a way," we sang together, "to get back homeward." "Golden Slumbers" was one of my favorite tracks on the album, but as I sang it that day, the words held a newer, deeper significance.

"Once there was a way to get back home." I tried to hide my face from my dad as I sang these words, the tears sliding down my face. I wiped my cheeks and quickly looked at him to see if he had noticed my tears, only to find that he was crying as well. He looked at me, and we both half smiled and continued to sing louder and louder, "Boy, you've got to carry that weight, carry that weight a long time!"

Finally the album was over, and my throat was hoarse from all the singing. My dad looked at me and said, "I'm glad you're here, buddy."

"Thanks."

SK8-R-Die

The next few months were pretty much the same: My dad still fought his depression with occasional sing-along sessions with his favorite records, I still was not on speaking terms with my mom, and I saw my brothers and sister occasionally when they came over to visit or stay the night. The biggest change in my life was that I was now a freshman at Bear River High School. The transition was easy for me, and it was nice to have a place to go during the daytime. At lunch the first day I found the God Squad. As we got in line to buy the school lunch, we quickly determined where our regular lunch spot would be because the tables were filling up fast.

Emote Control

Betty, our lunch lady at the high school, was an odd bird. We had heard that due to some freak cooking accident years before, she had burned her eyebrows off, and they never grew back. So for years Betty had to draw eyebrows on her face. Unfortunately, she had never become skilled at drawing consistent eyebrows. Every day when she filled our plates, she had a new expression on her face. Some days she looked permanently surprised; some days she looked constantly angry; some days she had used the wrong pencil and came to work with blue eyebrows; some days she had painted one eyebrow higher than the other and looked like she was in a continuous state of investigation. We always joked that Betty had lost her emote control.

From that claimed perch we looked around at all the new faces (many of them with facial hair!) and wondered what the future held. As I looked out on that sea of faces, it was as if the clouds parted to make room for the sun's glorious rays. The crowd of people split in two, giving me a clear look at none other than Sunny Gersbach. Except something was different about her. Her beautiful glow had dimmed to a dull flicker. She was wearing combat boots, big, baggy skater pants, and a SK8-R-Die black T-shirt. She was surrounded by skater punks and appeared to be talking to them as if they were friends.

What have they done to my Sunny? I asked myself as my eyes practically bugged out of my head. *What have the skaters done to my flawless Sunny? They've tainted perfection. They've tainted perfection!* Melodrama was oozing from every pore of my body as I looked at my beautiful woman, now a victim of skater society.

"There are other fish in the sea," Nater said as he read my facial expression and saw what I was looking at. He patted my back reassuringly, looking off in the distance at Sunny and her skater posse, and said, "She doesn't know what she's missing."

"Yeah, right," I said. We finished our school lunches and chatted about what we had done during the summer. The bell rang all too soon, and we headed off to the rest of the day's classes. I watched Sunny disappear into the crowd and wondered who or what would fill this new void in my life.

9

My Getaway Car

My fourteenth birthday finally arrived that crisp, sunny day in late October. I'd always had a love-hate relationship with that time of year; I loved that my birthday was coming up, but I hated that daylight-saving time was about to end. I hated the shorter days when I would return home from school, and it would already be dark outside. Any outdoor activities were basically on hold until spring.

A few of my teachers wished me a happy birthday, and some of my classmates said "happy birthday" in passing, but the day was nothing spectacular. At lunchtime Betty stuck a single birthday candle in my mac and cheese. "I'd light it for you, but Hunter would never allow an open flame in the cafeteria," the lunch lady said. Hunter was the high-school security officer who took his job as a rent-a-cop far too seriously.

In Security

Hunter had graduated from Bear River High School five years earlier and quickly fell in the "loser" category when he took the job as campus security. However, apparently no one told him, because campus

security was not to be messed with. Coke machines were not to be
kicked, students were not to go to their cars for any reason whatsoever, only five people were allowed in the rest rooms at a time, and
absolutely no open flames were permitted. He would constantly hit on
the ag girls in hopes of scoring a date but struck out most of the
time.

The thing that really intrigued me about Hunter was his name. I
mean, if you're naming your son Hunter, then why not call his brother
Gatherer? or Plumber? or Mechanic?

I smiled and secretly thought that Betty probably didn't want to
light the candle because she was afraid she might singe some other
hair on her head.

The God Squad gathered around our normal lunch table, and
everyone wished me a happy birthday.

"Got a present for you," Aaron said.

"Oh, you didn't have to do that," I said.

In Spite of You

Why do we feel like we have to say that when people hand us gifts?
The truth of the matter is, if they are close friends or family, then,
yes, they did have to do that. If they didn't, you'd remember the next
time their birthday rolled around, and you would buy them a gift out
of spite in hopes that they would remember they hadn't bought you a
present on your birthday. It's a twisted world out there.

I opened up the present to discover a wall calendar of the Beatles.

"Thanks, man. This is great," I said.

"Here, this is from me." T-bone handed me a long tube and box.

I opened up the tube first and discovered it was the poster of *Sgt. Pepper's Lonely Hearts Club Band.*

"Awesome!" I said.

"Open the box, too," T-bone said.

I opened it and found a pair of old kneepads.

"So you don't ever skin your knees again if somebody knocks you on the blacktop," he said with a half smile.

I laughed and thanked him for the thoughtful gifts.

"Here you go, man." Nater pulled a present from his backpack.

I opened the gift, and inside the shoebox were four Russian matrioshka dolls, each with an image of one of the Beatles.

Back in the USSR

A matrioshka doll is made of wood and opens up to reveal a smaller doll. When that doll is opened, there is another smaller doll, and so on. The name *matrioshka* comes from the Russian word for "mother," *mat* (taken from the Latin root *mater*). The suffix, oshka, is frequently used in Russian to denote a diminutive and endearing form of a name. A literal interpretation of the term *matrioshka* could be "little mother."

"Oh, dude," I said, "these are great! Where did you find them?"

"I got them for you when we went to Ukraine this summer." Nater and his dad had gone on a two-week trip to Ukraine doing humanitarian work. "They love the Beatles over there."

"Wow, I don't even know what to say."

"Here you go." Stick awkwardly slid a brown paper bag across the table. I opened the bag and pulled out a small, clear plastic box. The other guys looked closely, as none of us could quite figure out what it was.

"It's a *heteronychus arator*," Stick explained as we all looked at each other and shrugged. "A black beetle. I found it on our property, and I know you like beetles."

We all looked at one another, trying not to laugh. In fact, that's exactly what it was—a black beetle with a pin shoved through it sitting in a small, plastic display box.

"Wow," I said. "Thanks, Stick. Very thoughtful." We all chuckled and passed the beetle around to get a closer look at Stick's contribution.

"Nice," Aaron said. "Looks like your Beatles collection just doubled in one fowl swoop."*

---

*Correct saying: One fell swoop
Definition: Doing something in a single period of activity, usually swiftly

---

I smiled, looked over at Aaron, and said, "Fell!"

"Who fell?" Aaron asked.

"The swoop," I said.

"Who?" Aaron looked thoroughly confused.

"No," I said, seeing that I wasn't getting through. "Who's on first."

Nine Presents

My sister, Joy, didn't have basketball practice that afternoon, so she gave me a ride back to my dad's place.

"When are you going to move back home?" she asked as we pulled into the parking lot of the apartment complex. "We all miss you there. Mom really misses you too."

"I don't know," I said. "It's complicated."

Actually, it wasn't. When it came right down to it, the reason I wasn't moving back into the house was that I was too proud to apologize to my mom for cussing her out and totally disrespecting her.

"Think about coming back home," Joy said as she fought back the urge to cry.

"Okay," I said.

We parked and walked into my dad's apartment.

"Hey, happy birthday, buddy!" my dad said as we came through the door. My sister went over and gave him a hug and a kiss. All my brothers were sitting on the couch watching TV and talking about the day's events. The smell of bacon and eggs filled the tiny apartment.

"Who's up for a little breakfast for dinner?" my dad asked.

We all grabbed a plate, served up our dinner, and sat around my dad's apartment. It had been a long time since we had shared a meal together, and it was great to have everyone there. I looked around as we ate our bacon, eggs, and toast and noticed that almost everyone had cut up the bacon and eggs and were scooping it onto their toast, just like Mom always did. This small gesture turned my mom's absence into a cavernous void that evening. I hadn't spoken to her in months, and I missed her badly. I had such strange, mixed emotions about her. I wanted Mom back, but I also hated her for putting me through all of this and for kicking me out of the house. Occasionally I still felt angry toward my dad, but when we could sit down and talk about music or listen to records, we found a connecting point, and I was reminded again that he was still my dad. Since I hadn't been speaking to Mom, it was easy to forget she was still my mom and not just some villain who lived a mile away.

We finished eating, and I opened a few gifts from my brothers and sister. The gifts were small and thrifty—a homemade card, a record needle, a couple of mix tapes. With the family's money so tight, it really was the thought that mattered. The nice evening made me realize I missed just hanging out with my siblings as we had done for so many years.

"Here, this is from Mom," Joy said as she handed me a gift in the shape of a book.

"Oh," I said awkwardly. I opened it up to find a black leather journal inside. "Cool," I said.

I opened to the first page of the journal, and on it were written the words "To collect your thoughts. I love you. Mom."

"Well, I've gotta jet," Joy said about seven o'clock. "I have to write a government paper tonight, and I've got zero-period basketball practice tomorrow."

"Okay," my dad said as all of my brothers packed up their stuff since my sister was their ride. "Well, it was great having everybody here."

All my brothers gave Dad a hug except for Jeffrey (he just tolerated my dad putting his arms around him), and they all wished me a happy birthday.

"Think about coming home," Joy said as she gave me a parting hug.

"Okay," I said, and they filed out the door and into Joy's car.

"Tell Mom thanks for the journal," I said as Joy opened the driver's-side door.

"I will," she shouted back.

My dad closed the door, and I headed back to my room to start my homework.

"Hey," my dad said, "where are you going, buddy?"

"I've got to do some homework."

"Well, don't you want to open your present from me?" he asked.

"Oh," I said surprised, "I didn't think that…" Since the money had completely stopped coming in and my dad was broke, I was sure he had forgone a present this year.

"You thought I wouldn't get you something?" he said. "Sit down on the couch, and I'll be out in a second."

I sat down on the couch and turned off the TV. I wondered what my dad could have gotten me. He returned with eight packages and put them on the coffee table in front of me. I grabbed the top package and ripped it open to find a music book.

"*Billy Joel's Greatest Hits!* This is great!" I wasn't exactly sure what I was going to do with it, but it was still cool. I tore through several others to find music book anthologies by Elton John, James Taylor, Paul Simon, and the Beatles.

"Sweet!" I said. "Now I can know every word to every song."

"Open the other ones," my dad said with a grin.

I tore open the next package and wasn't sure what the object inside was. Apparently my expression conveyed that.

"It's a capo," Dad said. "It's for changing the key on a guitar."

"Oh cool," I said. "Nater was telling me about these." Nater had both an acoustic and an electric guitar at his place, and when I went to his house, I strummed a few chords on one of the guitars.

I opened the last gift and found a small plastic bag full of little multicolored pieces of hard plastic.

"It's a bag of all my old guitar picks," Dad said. I knew my dad had played guitar years ago, but I hadn't seen him pick one up since I was very little. "I thought you might like those."

"Cool," I said as I pulled out some mother-of-pearl picks. "Thanks,

Dad." By this time I had noticed the obvious theme but was sure all of this wasn't leading to what I wanted but could not expect.

"Okay, now close your eyes," he said as he walked down the hall toward his bedroom. "Are they closed?"

"Yeah, they're closed."

"Okay," he said, his voice coming toward me this time. "You can open them."

I opened my eyes and looked down at the floor at a big, black guitar case.

"What…" I couldn't begin to fathom where my dad had gotten this.

"Open it up," he urged.

I unlatched the case and saw an old, beat-up acoustic guitar inside.

"Where did you get this?" I asked as I pulled it out.

"It's my old guitar. Your mother gave it to me as a wedding present years ago, and now I want you to have it."

I was speechless. I ran my hands over the dented wood and the dusty strings. "I love it!"

"Now you can learn to play all your favorite songs on the guitar," he said with a smile from ear to ear.

I didn't know what to say. I thought about everything my dad had been through that year. This was incredible! The fact that with very little money he still found a way to give me the greatest birthday presents I had ever received was truly mind blowing.

He gave me the gift of music.

For the remainder of the evening, we sat in the living room, playing music and singing songs. My dad showed me some basic chords and strumming patterns on the guitar.

"Ahh, look at all the lonely people," we sang together. "Ahh, look at all the lonely people." But that evening there were no lonely people to be found. The apartment living room became a cathedral of music. We were two broken people singing our pain through the melody and harmony and through the major and minor chords.

10

Not the Place
They Intended
This to End

T he week after my birthday was a good one. I couldn't wait to get back to my dad's place to play the guitar and learn more chords so I could play new songs. It was the opportunity I had been waiting for: I was now an active participant. I was making music...or at least something that slightly resembled music. When I got home from school, I'd head straight for my room, pick up the guitar, and play until my fingers could stand it no longer. I loved every second of it.

Joy's proposition weighed heavily on me after my birthday, and I knew I had to make things right with my mom. That following Saturday afternoon I slipped out of my dad's apartment and walked back to the place I used to call home. Huffing up the driveway, I noticed little details about every part of the house: the spot in the front yard where we buried the dead bird we found, the broken bushes where my dad ate it on the go-cart, the patches of poison oak where we retrieved our poorly shot basketballs, the rocking chairs on the deck where my mom used to read to us. All of these memories flooded back as I approached the front door. I raised my index finger to ring the bell, but John and Joseph had seen me approaching and were running to let me in.

When they opened the door, the smell of our house brought a flood of memories.

"What are you doing here?" John asked excitedly.

"Is Mom here?" I asked, but before they could answer, she came around the corner and grabbed me tightly. I squeezed back as hard as I could and tried several times to open my mouth and say the words, "I'm sorry," but the words seemed redundant. The hug was already saying them.

After a few minutes we finally let go and sat down in the family room.

"So how are things?" Mom asked.

"Okay," I said.

"Did you like your birthday present?" she asked.

"Yeah, I loved it."

"Have you journaled in it at all?"

"No, not yet," I replied. "I don't really know what I would say. It seems like there is so much that I don't know where to start."

"Don't worry," she said. "It will all come to you at some point."

We sat and talked for a while, and I told her about the guitar and the music books and showed her how raw my fingertips were from playing so much.

"That's great," she said. "I saved for a long time to get your dad that guitar." My stomach knotted when she said that. Just the thought of that guitar being a token of my parents' love for each other was a strange irony. "It's a nice guitar, so make sure to take care of it."

"I will."

"You know, we never meant for it to end up this way, your father and I."

"Yeah," I said as I diverted my eyes to the ground. Except the thing was, I *didn't* know that they never meant for it to end this way.

"It's not like we got married and thought, *Well, hope this sticks.* We got married with the intent of staying together forever, and we gave it the best shot we possibly could."

It was an obvious statement, but for some reason it had never occurred to me. In my mind it was as if my parents had planned on staying married until it was no longer convenient and then headed in separate directions—no matter who was hurt in the process.

"We never meant to hurt you kids, and it makes me sick to see you all hurting." As she finished this statement, I could no longer contain the burn in my eyes and started to cry. It felt good to cry in the arms of my mother.

"Can I come back home now?" I asked.

"If you want to," she said. "But I think being with your dad has been good for you and good for him. Maybe you should split your time between our places for a while and see how it goes."

Drown Out the Battle Sounds

I moved half of my stuff back into my room and decided to split my time as best I could between the house and my dad's apartment. It was nice because I felt I was able to get the best of both worlds. But I was definitely getting the worst of both worlds too.

After six months of separation, my parents were trying to figure out the next step. I think everyone knew it was to file for divorce, but making that huge decision is not as easy as just speaking it.

Sometimes my dad would come over to the house to drop off one of the boys from soccer practice or just to visit, or Mom would go to Dad's apartment to drop off some mail or something he needed. It was completely predictable to everyone except them that these little visits would always turn into giant blowouts behind closed doors. The fighting was like before they had separated, except now it was worse, more heated.

My sister was often at basketball practice and didn't have to deal with the fighting on a firsthand basis. Jeffrey had gotten to the point where he would come home, grab the cordless telephone and a snack, and go into his room for the rest of the evening. The younger boys still watched TV at high volume to try to drown out the battle sounds. As for me, whenever these eruptions occurred, I would go into my room, close the door, and grab that beat-up guitar. I would start with *The Beatles Anthology* and play the songs cover to cover, trying to teach myself the chords. I would then tear through the James Taylor, Elton John, Billy Joel, Paul Simon, Sting, and Stevie Wonder music books. The more my parents fought, the better I got at playing guitar. The day I finally could play and sing at the same time brought a whole new level of passion to those evenings. All the songs I had listened to in order to escape my parents' fighting now became the songs I sang to drown out the shouting.

I would close my eyes and sing those songs with everything I had in me. Music was my sanctuary. That old, beat-up guitar—once a symbol of Mom's love for Dad—became my getaway car from the battle that raged down the hall. It was my tool to turn pain into passion, misery into music.

With every strum, I was transported to another place and time. A place where Sgt. Pepper and the Rocket Man sat side by side sharing stories of war and outer space. A place where Reggae Woman could boogie all night, Julio could be down by the schoolyard, Sweet Baby James could go to Carolina in his mind, and Gordon Sumner could watch every breath you take. A place where we would all join the Piano Man singing "la de da da de da, la de da da de da da dum." A place where I ruled as commander in chief with a guitar pick in my hand and a song on my lips.

A place where I was known simply as Six String Rocketeer.

Four

Years

Later

11

Life as It Happens

While the phone rang persistently in my freshman dorm room, I kicked a pathway through all the dirty laundry on the floor. "Hello," I said, hoping the caller was still there after seven rings.

"Hey, buddy." It was my dad. His voice had a sad tone.

"What's going on?" I asked.

"Well, I'm not exactly sure how to tell you this." My stomach tensed up as if I were expecting a swift punch to the gut. "Granddad passed away this evening."

"What?" I asked in disbelief, tears filling my eyes at the thought of never seeing him again. "How?"

"His heart just stopped. It was sudden, and he didn't feel any pain," he tried to console me.

We stayed on the phone and cried for a while. After I had regained control of my emotions, we talked about the logistics of the funeral.

"You, Joy, and I will fly out to Pennsylvania in a couple of days for the funeral," he explained. "Jeffrey, John, and Joseph will stay with your mom."

"Okay." We said our good-byes and hung up.

I looked around the disheveled dorm room and wondered how I would find enough clean clothes for the trip. I also wondered how I had made such a mess of the dorm room in my first two weeks of college.

The Ninth Hole

My sister, who was attending the same college, and I flew out of Los Angeles and met our dad in Pennsylvania. My dad's sister, Gayle, and my dad's uncle Chester were waiting for us at the airport. After hellos, hugs, and "My, look how grown-up you are!" in thick Pennsylvania accents, we piled into Uncle Chester's Cadillac and headed over to Granddad's place to freshen up.

> *Name: Chester Butterworth*
> *AKA: Uncle Chester*
> My great-uncle Chester was a lively one. He lived
> in Florida and made his living as a funeral home director.
> His love for nice cars, watercolor art, dapper clothes,
> Miami beach, and Liza Minnelli—combined with the
> fact that he was a lifelong bachelor—had always raised
> eyebrows. These facts about Chester never troubled
> us. He was a hilarious guy who worked with the dead,
> lived life to the fullest, and either spoke his mind or
> didn't speak at all.

Name: *Gayle Butterworth*
AKA: *Aunt Gayle*
Stats: My aunt Gayle is a career teacher who loves her students, her cats, and her soap operas. She tapes every
episode of her favorite soaps during the day and watches
them in the evening to catch up on the day's happenings.
Her pretty, long red hair is impossible to miss, and her hugs
never last less than a minute. She is a great gift giver and
never misses a birthday or Christmas, even though she
hasn't spent one with us in years. Behind the tough, East
Coast accent, she is a tender soul who loves to love.

It was good to see them both. We didn't get to see my dad's side
of the family very often since we lived so far away.

"He was on the ninth hole of the miniature golf course when he
went down." Uncle Chester explained to us how Granddad had died.
Because of his line of work, death was something Chester dealt with
daily, and he talked about it like he was describing his favorite cheese
spread. "After your grandmom Caroline passed away several years ago,
he started going out every week with a social club. You know, movies,
card games, tango dancing—that type of thing. Anyway, this week
they were playing mini golf down by the mall."

I was glad to hear that my granddad was still out and about in his
old age.

"When it was his turn, he stepped right up to the tee, dropped
his golf ball in its spot, lined up his putt, and then looked up at his

friends and said, 'Oh my.' The next thing you know, he fell over like a redwood tree. Dead before he hit the ground."

It was not the most tactfully told tale, but it was good to know that Granddad had died having fun.

"So when we go to the viewing tonight, he may have some cuts and scrapes on his cheeks and forehead from the fall," Uncle Chester explained.

Uncle Chester parked his Caddy in front of Granddad's place, and we headed inside. I hadn't been there in almost five years, and as I looked around, I couldn't find any evidence that time had passed. Everything in the house seemed exactly the same. The place gave me a weird feeling of sadness mixed with spookiness.

After we changed and freshened up, we got back in Uncle Chester's pride and joy and headed to the funeral home for the family's viewing of Granddad.

"Now don't forget," Chester prepped us as we were escorted into the parlor where Granddad's body lay. "His face may be a little scratched from the fall, but I'm sure they did everything they could to cover it with makeup."

The double doors swung open slowly, and there, lying in the casket across the room, was my granddad, the original William Jesse Butterworth.

Name: William Jesse Butterworth Sr.
AKA: Bill Senior, Big Bill, or Granddad
Stats: Granddad was a lovable old man of few words. We always knew that thousands of stories were creeping

around behind those eyeballs, but it was like pulling teeth to get him to tell one. He had lived through the Great Depression, fought in World War II, and worked on the railroad for forty-one years. But the only thing he ever wanted to talk about was what had happened on the most recent episodes of *MacGyver* and *Matlock*.

When he did speak, his voice sounded like a forced whisper. He had lost his voice box to throat cancer the year I was born, so I never knew what his normal speaking voice sounded like. Anyway, the loud whisper just added to his character.

It was always difficult to get anything but a muted reaction from him. For example, one year he spent Christmas with us, and we watched the Bill Murray movie *Scrooged* to get into the Christmas spirit. After the movie ended, we all looked at Granddad to get a read on what he thought of it. His gaze never left the TV screen as he said in his gruff, loud whisper, "Well, that was different."

I always found it odd that he would put butter on the bread of his ham and cheese sandwiches. He also loved fish sticks and would dip them into "tar tar" (that's the way he pronounced it) sauce.

His relationship with my dad wasn't much different from his relationship with us. You knew that he loved you, but you never knew how he might express it. He wasn't crazy about saying, "I love you," and hugs were only for initial hellos and final good-byes, but you just always knew (or at least assumed) that he loved you.

I hadn't seen Granddad since his last visit to California the year before, and it was strange to see him in that casket wearing his favorite blue blazer he'd bought in the Caribbean, his hair combed exactly the way he had combed it for sixty years, and his broad shoulders filling every inch of the box.

With every step I took toward his body, I came nearer and nearer to the realization that he was gone forever. My crying became uncontrollable. It was nearly impossible to connect the dots in my mind that Granddad's soul was gone forever and only his lifeless body remained. He looked as if he were sleeping and would awake at any minute to invite us all out to a Phillies' game. But, alas, he was gone.

STIFF AS AN OAR

After the tears had subsided, my dad, sister, aunt, great-uncle, and I stood around the casket and took a collective deep breath. After the initial shock of the moment, our attention immediately was drawn to his hands. Granddad's face was peaceful, and his big, broad body looked normal, but his thick arms and big hands extended awkwardly like two canoe paddles. Instead of one lying naturally over the other on his chest, rigor mortis had set in, and his arms were straight and stiff. His hands were wedged awkwardly at his side with the fingers fully extended. Granddad was a Frankenstein look-alike!

Dead Man Talking

Rigor mortis occurs a few hours after a person dies, because the joints of the body stiffen and lock in place. This phenomenon is caused by skeletal muscles that have partially contracted. Uncle Chester was telling us that all this was normal, but usually the mortician is able to make the body look a little more peaceful. He told us that the worst funeral experience of his career had happened a few months before. The wife of the deceased was paying her final respects as her husband lay in the coffin. As she leaned over to kiss his forehead, she put her hand against his chest and dislodged some air that had been trapped in his lungs. The air came through his throat, making it sound as if he had just said, "Ohhhhhhh!" in a deep eerie tone, causing all of the funeralgoers to scream and run for the doors in mass pandemonium.

"Well, that's just not going to do," Uncle Chester said, reaching into the coffin to readjust Granddad's arms. Joy and I immediately looked at each other. Was this something we should watch?

"Let's just cross these here like this and…" Uncle Chester, who was far too comfortable with dead bodies, was crossing Granddad's arms on his chest to make him look more natural. When he let go of Granddad's arms, they immediately shot back down to his sides.

"Ahhhhh!" we all screamed and stepped back as it appeared the corpse had moved on its own. My dad, Joy, and I stood back a couple of feet from the coffin with eyes as big as compact discs. While Uncle Chester contemplated his next move, Aunt Gayle began dry heaving in the corner.

"There's got to be a way," Uncle Chester said to himself as he fished through his pockets and pulled out a sewing kit. I thought it was very odd that Uncle Chester carried a sewing kit around in his pocket, but perhaps the funeral business required some occasional quick work with the needle. He took a safety pin out of the kit and grabbed both of Granddad's arms, forcing them together. "Billy," Uncle Chester said to my dad, "give me a hand here." Uncle Chester instructed my dad to hold Granddad's arms together over his stomach while he safety-pinned the cuffs of his shirt together, hoping to keep his arms in a less awkward position.

After Uncle Chester gave my dad the go-ahead, he let go of Granddad's arms, and they stayed in place on his stomach. "Much better…" Just as Uncle Chester said this, the safety pin gave up the ghost and broke in half, and my Granddad's arms shot back to his sides.

"Hmmm…" Uncle Chester looked puzzled. "If I had my kit here, I'd be able to get his arms to stay down." My dad, trying to avoid another freak-show moment, convinced Uncle Chester just to let it go. This was obviously a hard thing for him to shake off, not only because it was his brother in that box, but also because his line of business was to make dead people look good.

"Well," Uncle Chester said as he looked at Granddad, "at least they did a good job on his face."

ETERNALLY GRATEFUL

The funeral service was the next day, and we all came dressed in our best suits or dresses. As we greeted total strangers at the door of the funeral home, we were regaled with story after story of how great a man our granddad was—how he had volunteered his time to drive senior citizens to their doctors' appointments, dished up food at the local soup kitchen, read aloud to children once a week at the local library, and been an elder in his church. All of this was news to us, but it made us even prouder to have him as our granddad.

Per my granddad's wishes, Dad gave the eulogy. I'm not sure how he was able to stand next to the body of his father and talk about his life so poignantly without completely losing it, but he did a fantastic job.

"I remember a time when I was helping my dad repair a leak in the attic," my dad said from behind a podium covered with white lilies. "I was probably about eight years old at the time and was so excited to be helping my dad. I watched as he meticulously put each tool back into its proper place in the toolbox after its use. As he was grabbing a couple of screws out of the hardware compartment, he dropped one, and it started rolling away. 'Don't worry, Dad. I'll get it,' I said as I lunged forward to grab it. Unbeknown to me, the floor was unfinished where I was about to step. If I had planted my foot there, I would have dropped straight through the ceiling and landed in our downstairs kitchen.

" 'Whoa, buddy,' my dad said as he grabbed me before I could fall and hurt myself. 'Watch your step there, buddy.' And even though he didn't say the words 'I love you' at that moment, I knew that was what he was telling me with his actions."

Tears flowed, and Kleenexes were passed as we watched my dad turn from the podium to face Granddad in his coffin and say, "I love you, too, Dad."

As my dad told this story, the thought occurred to me that I had never needed to read between the lines with my parents. No matter what was happening in their lives, I always knew beyond a shadow of a doubt that my parents were still absolutely, 100 percent crazy about me, and they never had a problem telling me or showing me. And for that knowledge, I am eternally grateful.

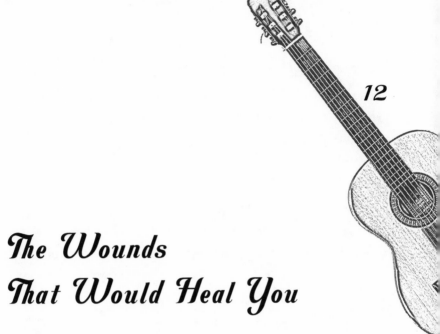

The Wounds That Would Heal You

I returned to college after the funeral and felt like I was not in a healthy place in my life. The funeral had opened up old wounds in my heart that I needed to deal with. I knew I had to make my peace with God and deal with my parents' divorce.

It was such a daunting task, though, and I didn't have any clue how I was going to do either of these things. For months I tried to run away from it by drinking, dating, shopping, reading, working, playing, and listening to music, but one February night it all caught up with me.

I was playing my beat-up guitar and thumbing through the pages of *James Taylor's Greatest Hits* music book that Dad had given me years before. Some of the pages had come loose from the binding, and the ones still in place were bent and worn from use. I finished singing "Walking Man" and turned the page to the James Taylor classic "Fire and Rain."

I was playing and singing the song as I had done hundreds of times before, but this time I stopped dead in my tracks when I reached the lyrics "Won't you look down upon me, Jesus. You've got to help me make a stand." I couldn't bring myself to sing these words, because this time they weren't just words on a page. They were my heart's cry. I debated whether to turn the page and keep going, but I felt like I was at a crossroads. I could continue running away or start running toward Him. During all these months when I'd thought about getting right with God but had had no idea what to say, my redemption song was sitting right in front of me in the form of James Taylor's "Fire and Rain."

 I Always Thought That I'd See You Again

Rumor has it that James Taylor wrote the song "Fire and Rain" after a friend whom he had met in rehab committed suicide after almost coming clean.

"Won't you look down upon me, Jesus," I sang as my throat tightened up with emotion, and tears filled my eyes. "You've got to help me make a stand."

After I sang those words, I broke down and cried and promised God that from that day on, I was His and only His if He would have me. It was the first prayer I had offered since I'd prayed underneath those manzanita trees, but this time I was certain that God heard me.

THE SECOND THOUGHT

In the weeks after I reconciled with God, I still had a nagging feeling that there was a gaping wound in my soul that needed attention. Months earlier, when I was at Granddad's funeral, I had walked to the bathroom to wash my face. On the way there I saw a plaque hanging in the hallway of the funeral home. It read:

The Funeral:
Helps confirm the reality and finality of death.
Provides a climate for mourning and the expression of grief.
Is a celebration for a life that's been lived
as well as a sociological statement that a death has occurred.

I only skimmed the plaque on the way to the bathroom. On the way back I gave it a good hard look. What was it about the plaque that bothered me?

Now back at college, I felt that I was handling Granddad's death appropriately through grieving and mourning. But one day as I sat in my Music Fundamentals class (we always called it Fun-for-Mentals), I finally made the connection of why the words on that plaque had stuck with me. On the subconscious level I understood that sign not as if it was talking about the death of a person but rather the death of a relationship. *A divorce.*

I had stayed mostly silent about my parents' divorce for years, thinking I was cool with it because time had worn down most of the sharp edges. But the truth was that I had never fully come to terms with the beast that was the divorce. I knew I had to do something about it, so I made an appointment with the college counselor to see if he could shed a little light on the matter.

I sat in the waiting room of the counselor's office, praying that no one I knew would walk by, recognize me, and ask what I was doing there. I'm not sure why I was ashamed. I suppose at some point I had picked up the idea that talking to a counselor meant admitting that you are weak and can't figure out your problems on your own. At that point in my life, that was exactly right. I couldn't figure out my problems on my own, and I needed a fresh, professional perspective on my life.

I picked up an old copy of *People* magazine and starting reading an article about what kinds of treats the cast of the sitcom *Friends* fed their beloved pets.

"Anyone sitting here?" a female voice inquired as she pointed to the seat across from me.

"No, be my guest," I said as I motioned toward the seat.

A woman in her early thirties sat down and snapped, "Memo, get away from there!" She was talking to her four-year-old son, Memo, who was trying to shove the dirt from a potted plant into the electrical socket on the wall.

"Mommy," Memo said, "I'm hungry."

"Okay," the woman responded as she looked over the book she had started to read. "Come and get it, then."

The reason I'm telling you this part of the story is not because it has anything to do with my story but because what happened next was so bizarre.

"Okay," Memo said, and he walked over to his mother, lifted up her shirt, and stuck his head underneath it. I immediately averted my eyes, but the woman didn't flinch a muscle.

"No, not that one," she said. "You had that one last time." Memo's head moved from one side of her shirt to the other as he began to feed from his mother's breast.

"Owww!" his mother said as she flicked the back of his head through her shirt. "Don't bite!"

"William Butterworth," the receptionist called out just in the nick of time.

"Yeah, that's me," I said as I got up quickly, threw the magazine to the ground, and rushed away from milking Memo and his uninhibited mommy. Walking into the counselor's office, I decided that maybe my problems weren't as bad as I thought they were.

MOURNING HAS BROKEN

My counseling appointment was a resounding success. It wasn't that I had a major breakthrough, but just to have someone sit there and know the right questions to ask and then listen to my responses was a cathartic experience.

His biggest advice was to let myself mourn the death of my parents' marriage the same way I was allowing myself to mourn the death of my granddad. He really encouraged me to journal as much as I could and to get my thoughts and feelings down on paper.

So I took his advice and dug up the old journal my mom had given me for my fourteenth birthday. I hadn't written a word in it, but I had always kept it with my music books just in case inspiration struck. I remembered Mom telling me that the words to fill the pages of the journal would come in time. That time had arrived.

I carried the journal with me everywhere I went for the next couple of weeks and would just write and write whenever anything that vaguely resembled a thought or emotion came to mind. With every word that flowed through the pen onto those journal pages, it was as if the weight in my soul was now occupying those pages.

For weeks I continued journaling, seeing my counselor, and asking God to help me release the ghosts that still haunted me. One evening after finishing my Music Theory 101 homework, I found myself in a usual position: sitting in my dorm room holding my beat-up guitar, the songbooks in front of me. Except this time, instead of playing through the songbooks, I felt like the guitar in my hands was ready to tell a story.

I grabbed the capo Dad had given me years ago and fastened it tightly on the third fret of the guitar. I opened the journal that Mom had given me and plopped it on my desk. I began to play a chord progression that I'd been toying with for a while and noticed some phrases from my journal:

caught in the crossfire as the battle raged down the hall

As I pored over my journal, thoughts and phrases kept leaping from the page, begging to be sung.

My getaway car is this beat-up guitar.

My eyes ran over the pages as the words stepped forward.

The wounds were deep inside my soul.

For hours I collected those words and put them on their own pages. Through this process of playing and reading, singing and writing, a song took form.

By the end of the evening that once-white piece of paper was covered with my sweat and tears. A song was born.

"I finally did it," I said to myself. "Let the healing begin."

My thumb ran over the callused fingertips of my left hand as I mused at how far I'd come as a musician in the last four years—playing that guitar until my fingers bled, trying to train my hand to do what my mind was willing it to do, learning to strum with one hand and chord with the other. That guitar in my hands had been collecting dust for years until I was able to breathe new life into it—and it into me.

It occurred to me that I never would have had the discipline to learn to play the guitar if the divorce had not driven me into that room. If I had not spent those hours teaching myself how to play the guitar, I never would have written this song. And if I'd not written this song, I might still be looking for healing from the divorce.

It truly is remarkable to me that although I had no regard for God during the divorce, He was providing me with a way to cope through a beat-up guitar, a pile of music books from a brilliant army of musicians, and a voice that was dying to sing about something beautiful.

I smiled at those words on the page and was reminded of that quote all those years ago in Mr. Grant's English class: "The wounds that hurt you would be the wounds that would heal you." And at that moment I couldn't have agreed more.

Six String Rocketeer

CAUGHT IN THE CROSSFIRE
WHILE THE BATTLE RAGED DOWN THE HALL
THERE WERE NO BAD GUYS
JUST A COUPLE CONSENTING ADULTS
I JUST HAD TO GET AWAY
BUT I HAD NO CAR TO DRIVE
SO MY BODY STAYED INSIDE MY ROOM
AS I SLIPPED INTO MY MIND...

Chorus

I'M GOING OUT WHERE NO ONE CAN FIND ME
BEYOND THIS THICKENED AIR, ~~WHERE MY SOUL FLYS FREE~~
WHERE MY SPIRIT IS FREE

I'M ~~BREAK~~ BLASTING OFF WITH A STRUM OF
MY SIX STRING...
SIX STRING ROCKETEER

LIFE AS IT HAPPENS
IS RARELY THE WAY ~~THAT~~ YOU PLANNED
ROLL WITH THE PUNCHES
OR YOU'LL END UP A MAD LITTLE MAN...

STR

A BROKEN HOME WAS NOT THE PLACE
THEY INTENDED THIS TO END

~~ROCK THE CRIB POW DEEP~~ INSIDE MY SOUL
BUT THE WOUNDS WERE DEEP
LET THE HEALING BEGIN...

Chorus

BRIDGE:

I ~~STEP~~ ON BOARD, AS COMMANDER
IN CHIEF
~~THE BEATLES~~ SGT. PEPPER IN MILITARY MOTIF
WITH
WE WALK THE SHIP AND I NOD WITH A GRIN ~~SMILE~~
AT MY FRIENDS GORDON SUMNER AND
MUDSLIDE SLIM

"TAKE ME TO THE PILOT!" I DEMAND
AND THEY LEAD ME INTO THE ROCKET MAN
"WHO IS NAVIGATING?" I INQUIRE
AS JULIO SWEEPS DOWN BY THE SCHOOLYARD
~~xxxxxxxxxxxxxxxxxxxx~~
THERE MY SOUL WAS AS LIGHT AS A ~~FEATHER~~
AS THE PIANO MAN HAD US ALL
SINGING TOGETHER...

* Sting
* Billy Joel
* Elton John
* Beatles
* Paul Simon
* James Taylor

?

SIX STRING ROCKETEER

Verse 1

Caught in the crossfire
While the battle raged down the hall
There were no bad guys
Just a couple consenting adults.
I just had to get away
But I had no car to drive,
So my body stayed inside my room
As I slipped into my mind.

Chorus

I'm going out where no one can find me
Beyond this thickened air, where my spirit is free.
I'm blasting off with a strum of my six string
Six String Rocketeer.
Well, my getaway car is this beat-up guitar,
And I'm off, I'm off to that place
Where I find my escape.

Verse 2

Life as it happens
Is rarely the way that you planned.
Roll with the punches,
Or you'll end up a mad little man.
A broken home was not the place
They intended this to end.
But the wounds were deep inside my soul.
Let the healing begin.

Bridge

I step on board as commander in chief
With Sgt. Pepper in military motif.
We walk the ship and I nod with a grin
At my friends Gordon Sumner and Mudslide Slim.
"Take me to the pilot," I demand,
And they lead me into the Rocket Man.
"Who is navigating?" I inquire
As Julio swoops down by the schoolyard.
There my soul was as light as a feather
As the Piano Man had us all singing together.

Epilogue

T he whole family is gathered in one place this year. My wife, my
son, me. My mom is here, of course, as well as my dad and his
new wife. My sister, her husband and daughter, and all of my brothers and their significant others are under the same roof for the first
time since my parents split.

Honestly, I'm scared out of my mind that this whole celebration
will be a mess. Knowing me, I'll tell a joke that ends up revealing how
awkward I feel. And if no one says anything, that moment of uncom-
fortable silence just might devour any holiday cheer.

I hear my mom and dad talking about a movie they once saw
when they were married. I cringe. Any reminder that they were once
together and in love is an unwelcome trip down memory lane.

Don't you hate them for what they've done? Where did that thought
come from?

I look at my beautiful wife and remember how I almost broke it
off with her on multiple occasions before we got married, because I
was so afraid that our marriage would end in shambles.

*It happened to your parents. What makes you think it's not going to
happen to you?* There it is again; my self-doubt is acting up.

I look into the face of my infant son and imagine putting him
through a divorce that would leave him feeling confused, angry, iso-
lated, and burdened.

I'm sure your parents once held you as a baby and never intended to hurt you deeply. But look at what happened? You know it's going to happen again. Am I always going to live plagued by the uncertainty of when and how I'm going to blow up my marriage?

I look to my siblings and sense that they are as apprehensive and uneasy about this holiday as I am. I know the divorce still attaches its dirty tentacles to every one of our necks on almost a daily basis, squeezing mercilessly, hoping to alienate us from those we love.

∞

Do you feel the grip of those tentacles, even as you read these words?

Whenever you begin to feel constricted, be comforted by this thought: although the divorce will always have lingering effects, know that you are in the process of healing. This allows you constantly to break free of the lies bred by divorce.

And instead of believing those lies, you and I can embrace the truth: That Jesus has set us free from repeating the mistakes of our parents. That we are being healed by Him from the wounds of divorce. That we can have and grow relationships that are healthy and whole and lasting. This is the truth. And it sets us free.

∞

Back at the Christmas celebration, after I process this truth in my mind, I smile as I look around a room of broken people sincerely loving one another as best they can and continuing to journey down the road of healing.

Perhaps your family can't stand to be in the same room together, or maybe they aren't speaking to each other, or perhaps they constantly put on a happy face to mask the pain. Whatever your family dynamic, remember that healing is not a destination but rather a journey. When you allow yourself to take that road of restoration, only then do you begin to feel God's best for you.

Oh, and in case you are wondering, Christmas 2004 ended up being one of the best we've ever had.

Notes

Chapter 8: A Mad Little Man

1. The Beatles, "Golden Slumbers," *Abbey Road*, vinyl record, ©
   1959 Capitol/EMI.
2. The Beatles, "Carry That Weight," *Abbey Road*, vinyl record, ©
   1959 Capitol/EMI.

Chapter 9: My Getaway Car

1. The Beatles, "Eleanor Rigby," *Revolver*, vinyl record, © 1966
   Capitol/EMI.

Chapter 12: The Wounds That Would Heal You

1. James Taylor, "Fire and Rain," *Sweet Baby James*, vinyl record, ©
   1970 Warner Brothers.
2. Jesse Butterworth, "Six String Rocketeer," © Designer Music, a
   division of Zomba Enterprises, Inc. (SESAC). All rights for the
   world administered by Designer Music. Used by permission.

About the Author

From Gaelic to Gershwin, bluegrass to the Beatles, Jesse and his family have always been music enthusiasts. This diverse mixture of styles inspired Jesse and his siblings to write their own songs and perform them in whatever venue was available. Whether in the backyard, in the bedroom, in the bathtub, or on the beach, to Jesse, Joy, Jeffrey, John, and Joseph the world was a stage.

The Butterworth repertoire included such crowd favorites as "Prairie Girl Sweeps the Chimney," "Thexder! Thexder!" "Flowers in My Hair," "Dokey Broke My Water Bottle," and the perennial classic "Go to Church and Play Baseball." These songs birthed in Jesse a love for writing songs that continues today. Whether performing with Daily Planet, leading worship at Illuminate, or sitting by himself playing his beat-up guitar, Jesse is always listening for the next song in the soundtrack of his life.

Jesse lives in east Seattle with his wife, Marisa, and his son, Liam, and leads worship for Illuminate at Overlake Christian Church.

To listen to music samples, view his itinerary, or learn more about Jesse, log on to www.JesseButterworth.com.

Divorce isn't just an end—
it's also a beginning.

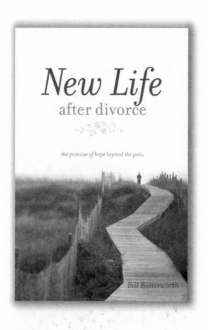

Learn to build a meaningful and joyful new life with the practical tools and spiritual insights of *New Life After Divorce*. Workbook also available.

Available in bookstores and from online retailers.

WATERBROOK PRESS
www.waterbrookpress.com